ENTERTAINING
in Style

GW00482765

Published by Bay Books
61-69 Anzac Parade,
Kensington NSW 2033.

Publisher: George Barber
Copyright © Bay Books

National Library of Australia
Card Number and ISBN 0 85835 971 5

The publisher would like to thank the following for their assistance
during the photography of this book: Cebu Cane, Kensington,
Peters of Kensington, Mikasa Tablewear, Stanley Rogers Silver
Cutlery, Kosta Boda, Fitz and Floyd, Armadillo for South American
Craft, Penfolds Wines, Australian Mushroom Growers'
Association.

Photography on page 27 was at the Quay Apartments, Sydney.
Managing Agent:
PRD Stanton Pty Ltd, 02 231 4055

Photography by John Garth
Front cover photo: Jon Macmichael
Food Styling by Elizabeth Carden and Karen Davidson
Printed in Singapore by Toppan Printing Co.

BB1286

ENTERTAINING
in Style

Compiled by Voula Kyprianou and Duske Teape-Davis
Entertaining ideas by Elisabeth King

BAY BOOKS
Sydney and London

CONTENTS

SECRETS OF SUCCESSFUL ENTERTAINING

Quail with Wild Rice

If some remarkable time machine could deliver the legendary Escoffier back to earth and deposit him in a modern push-button kitchen, it is doubtful whether he could prepare his own breakfast. The facts of cooking life have altered, and technology has given us things with which to work that were unknown a generation or two ago. And a good thing too. In the new age of food as news and across-the-board lack of time, nobody has the inclination to compete with a culinary shrine where squads of sous-chefs zap around refining stocks and stirring dozens of sauces.

Cooking ought to be in decline. Food science has made it possible for us all to eat without touching a raw ingredient. But in late 20th century Australia, at-home entertaining involving culinary skill and panache is in vogue. What isn't the style, are recipes adhering to the copper bowl-wire whisk syndrome and elaborate preparation.

This every-occasion entertaining cookbook bridges the gap between food guaranteed to whet the appetites of hosts and guests alike, and recipes well within a modern cook's time, scope and capabilities. Written in a clear and simple format, each menu looks good, tastes good and, very importantly, many of them can be prepared ahead of time. You'll find ideas for super lunches to small dinners, special occasion menus to big parties with small price tags, plus organising and preparation tips.

Roast Beef with Peppercorn Sauce

The do's and don'ts of successful entertaining

There are do's and don'ts involved in pulling off a successful party. The first do is to think of your expendable time. Always pick a menu where some or most of it may be made the day before. The second big do is to think of your expendable energy. Especially when baking, a lot of us get unnecessarily overworked. If you are going to the trouble of making yeast rolls, by all means arrange to have something on hand for dessert, such as home-made icecream you made the week before or a simple fruit concoction. The biggest don't, of course, is never overdo it. Let your guests leave glowing from a well-rounded meal.

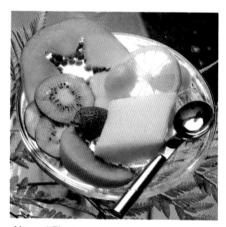

Almond Float

Shopping

To go food shopping without a list is to enter a battle of wits unarmed. An analogy that applies equally to working independently of a plan. Be organised for everything from equipment to shopping by following our precision time plans. Without exception, relaxed party givers write everything down — that means food, drink and even such details as buying candles and after-dinner chocolates. Another secret is to use only the finest, freshest ingredients — the best rarely needs embellishment.

Entertaining can be costly, but it doesn't have to be. There are a few tricks to being a gourmet chef on a budget, but they are easy to master. A good tip is to read local ads, then pick a menu that makes the most of what is on special at the moment. Good cuts of meat are always an expensive buy, but chicken has become the budget host's dream purchase. Pasta is a good choice for an entree, because it can be dressed up elegantly at little cost. Use the vegetables in season, anything from a turnip can be tarted up successfully, rather than buy a "fashion" legume which may set you back half the cost of the main course.

Time-saving techniques

Other time-saving techniques to follow are: clean up as you go along; read through each recipe again before starting to cook; wherever possible, double up on recipes and refrigerate or freeze for later use; and carefully review the recipes and note when the same ingredient must be readied for several recipes (chopped onion, minced parsley). Do all the preparation at once, then divide the ingredients and place on waxed paper.

Think of your freezer as a creative tool, not merely a storehouse for leftovers. Stockpile an assortment of ready-to-eat dishes and a variety of basic components, such as chopped herbs, fruit purees and creme patissiere for others. Then cash in your frozen assets whenever you need them. Even spur-of-the moment entertaining won't mean a mad dash to the shops.

Match the mood

Matching the menu with the table decor and even the mood throughout the house is one of the most enjoyable aspects of party planning. Special touches in menu and atmosphere really matter. Each person's inspiration for a table setting is entirely different, and that's where the fun comes in. And in case you're tempted to forget, fun is what entertaining should be.

For a French charcuterie buffet, few things work better than blue or green-rimmed heavy white porcelain plates on a green and white plaid tablecloth starred with a centrepiece of vivid red flowers, baskets of baguettes and huge white platters. A family dinner warms with pink rosebud china and lace-trimmed linen napkins. Instead of flowers, centre a huge basket of

Mediterranean vegetables for a Greek or Italian dinner. For a Chinese dinner, engender an oriental feeling with black or red plates and some black and white cotton napkins. A single white freesia in a glass sphere is pretty at each place.

When you're entertaining on a larger scale, the buffet is the easiest way to serve. The setting of a buffet table is an exercise in logic: the near end of the table is for the main course and plates, followed by vegetables, salad and bread; the far end of the table is for flatware and napkins. A buffet table should be a festive one. Mix and match plates, glasses and flatware. Leave the table bare if it is a splendid woodgrain; or cover with a "designer" sheet if you don't want to hire a basic white one. For effect, decorate with extra-long candles or grand cathedral holders.

Mix and match the menus

Just as the table setting shouldn't become a rigid formula, we don't expect you to follow our menus to the letter. You can, of course, but it's not obligatory. Create your own special menus by interchanging the recipes in our set formats. This gives you more flexibility with costing, time plans and effects — go cheaper and quicker, or more expensive and leisurely.

Cream of Oyster Soup

Wining and dining

The whole point of wine is enjoyment, never snobbery or fear. For special occasions there's nothing like "the bubbly". If your budget or the event doesn't stretch to imported French, happy alternatives are our own cheap and cheerfuls or the more up-market methode champenoise bottlings. For the best red and white selections, drink what you like or consult your local liquor stores.

Most red wines are best served at "cool room temperature". To let the wine breathe, uncork it at least half an

Hot Bean Dip

hour before dinner. Room temperature means 18°C (65°F), but as most homes are warmer than that, try to store wines in a cool place.

White and rosé wines should be chilled for at least two hours before serving. However, the finer the wine, the less chilling it needs as too much coldness ruins their delicate flavours. All champagnes should be served well chilled.

If you are serving two wines, you must have two separate wine glasses for each guest. A thin, clear glass is best. A tulip glass where the rim is narrower than the base of the bowl is the perfect choice, as it allows the bouquet of the wine to waft upward.

In general, two bottles is enough for four guests, but have a third standing by. Open three bottles for six to eight guests, have a fourth in reserve.

Putting people first

Up until now, all we've discussed is the food and wine, which are the basics of good entertaining, but not the only component of success. People really come first. If you always invite your old crowd, with no new faces, the conversation can become very repetitious. How often can you discuss school politics, office gossip, or even how your favourite rugby team is faring. Mix and match friends and acquaintances from the various circles of your life. New ideas bubble, new subjects are argued, people sit around the dining table long after the dishes are cleared, everything is more interesting and stimulating.

EK

The Preparation Timetables

To make entertaining easier, cut down on the last minute rush and help create the right mood for the meal, each menu includes a preparation timetable. This is simply a guide to preparing and cooking the food and doesn't include those other chores that must be attended to a day or so before a dinner party — cleaning the house, checking the table linen, crockery, cutlery and glassware.

Many recipes or part of a recipe in this book can be prepared in advance and frozen or stored in the refrigerator.

☐ This symbol means prepare to this point and heat or complete cooking just before serving.

Cooking ahead this way lets you make the most of any free time before the dinner party, leaving you cool, calm and completely ready when your friends arrive. A harassed host or hostess hardly sets the mood for an enjoyable evening. And there's little point in entertaining at all if you spend most of your time in the kitchen leaving your guests to entertain themselves.

Cold Citrus Chiffon

ENTERTAINING IN STYLE

Formal dinners don't have to be complicated, but the food must be rather special. Proving the point is our gourmet dinner for six. Few main courses are more spectacular and festive than Quail with Wild Rice. A similar rationale is the rich link between all of our "pamper yourself" menus, whether the meal is planned for eight, six, four, or two.

The first basic ingredient after selecting your menu, is to check your facilities to be sure that both your oven and surface cooking units are able to handle everything at once or sequentially. Also be sure your refrigerator or freezer can handle all the food (before and after cooking), ice and drinks. There's no point contemplating a dinner where every dish requires some sort of fridge space, if your refrigerator is slightly larger than a bar fridge. Small fridges stuffed to the gunwhales simply cannot cope with the heavy load — all dishes and wines stay at a temperature just below room temperature.

A touch of the unexpected makes a formal meal more dashing. It can be something like adding macadamia nuts to steamed rice, a mound of caviar to oyster soup, putting slivers of prosciutto in a dish of broccoli or decorating soft-boiled quail eggs with foie gras. Out of the ordinary ingredients are becoming commonplace in all major cities, for formal dinner parties it's a great idea to take advantage of the trend. Good hunting grounds are oontinental-style delicatessens, the ever-growing number of sophisticated food halls in department stores and ethnic markets and shopping areas.

All the world's a stage . . . especially formal dinner tables. Imaginative table settings are the lifeblood of upscale dinners. The lustre of silver and the dazzle of crystal provide a standard dream setting, but remember to polish everything to a mirror shine. A tete-a-tete for two can accommodate an avant-garde centrepiece of metal or simple stone sculpture softened with trailing greenery and simple porcelainware of deep primary colours.

If you want formal dinners for six to ten to have an old-world panache, decide if you need professional help. Catering firms will provide waiters and waitresses for fees that don't mean taking out a second mortgage. A duo of male and female creates a stunning impression. In the early stages, she can take coats and pass round the hors d'oeuvres, while he serves the aperitifs and arranges seating. During the meal, service is quicker and more special with two hands at the pump. Relentless romantics might even consider outside help for a dinner for two.

Similarly, if you want an aura of supreme elegance in table appointments, flatware and glasses, but don't want to go to the expense of buying expensive items that are used only rarely, hiring is again a good idea. Catering agencies will provide all you need for a small fee, which in many cases includes washing up and laundering.

Creamed Oysters and Prawns on Shell

DINING A DEUX

If there is someone special in your life and you are dining à deux, treat them to the following formal menu for two. Follow a platter of oysters with tender braised lamb fillets accompanied by snow peas.

MENU

Creamed Oysters and Prawns on Shell

Braised Lamb Fillets
Tomatoes Persilles
Snow Peas

Peach Ice Cream with Fresh Peaches and Madeleines

Served with Chardonnay

PREPARATION TIMETABLE

Prepare ahead and freeze: Ice cream for Peach Ice Cream. Store in a covered container. Do not prepare remaining peaches until day of dinner party.

2 days ahead: Bake Madeleines to serve with dessert. When cool, store in airtight container.

1 day ahead: Prepare lamb for Braised Lamb Fillets by trimming off excess fat and sinew. Cover and refrigerate. Trim Snow Peas of stalks. Rinse under cold water, drain and refrigerate in a plastic bag.

6 hours ahead: Prepare seafood for Creamed Oysters and Prawns on Shell. Refrigerate. Blanch Snow Peas, cover and refrigerate. Scoop ice cream for dessert into balls, place onto a metal slide covered with plastic wrap. Place plastic wrap over ice cream and return to freezer.

3 hours ahead: Finalise Creamed Oysters and Prawns on Shell. Arrange on a plate, cover with plastic wrap and refrigerate before baking. Prepare and fill tomatoes for Tomatoes Persilles. Place into greased baking dish cover and refrigerate. Blanch and pool remaining two peaches for dessert, slice and place into a bowl with syrup and Grand Marnier.

1 hour ahead: Prepare all garnishes. Cover with damp absorbent paper then wrap in plastic wrap and refrigerate.

30 minutes ahead: If desired, cook tagliatelle pasta to serve with lamb. Drain and keep warm in a colander over a saucepan of hot water.

15 minutes ahead: Bake Tomatoes Persilles. Pan fry lamb for Braised Lamb Fillets, cover with aluminium foil and keep in a warm (not hot) section of oven or grill. Prepare sauce for lamb.

Time for dinner: Bake or grill Oysters and Prawns on Shell. Garnish. Reheat Snow Peas by cooking gently in butter.

Left: Creamed Oysters and Prawns on Shell. Front: Braised Lamb Fillets with Snow Peas and Tomato Persilles

CREAMED OYSTERS AND PRAWNS ON SHELL

1 dozen fresh oysters in shell
125 g medium-sized raw prawns,
    shelled and deveined
50 g butter
½ cup fish stock
1½ tablespoons dry white wine
½ cup milk
1 tablespoon flour
1 egg yolk
¼ teaspoon white pepper
½ teaspoon salt
dash Tabasco
1 tablespoon soft white breadcrumbs
60 g Gruyère cheese, grated
lemon wedges and watercress
    for garnish

Lift oysters from shells and place on plate. Wash shells and dry. Remove any loose shell from oysters and cover them with damp greaseproof paper.

Melt 30 g butter in small frypan. Cook prawns 2–3 minutes until pink and just cooked. Remove, slice in half if too large, and keep warm.

Add fish stock to pan with the wine and simmer until reduced by ⅓. Strain and add to milk.

Melt 20 g butter, add 1 tablespoon flour and cook 1 minute. Add liquid and bring to the boil, stirring constantly. Beat the egg yolk in a bowl. Add a little of the hot sauce, then whisk the mixture into the remaining sauce. Reheat, but do not boil. Season with salt and pepper. Add the prawns.

Spoon a little sauce into the shells. Top with oysters; spoon sauce over the top. Sprinkle each with breadcrumbs and cheese mixture combined . ☐

Bake 4 minutes in a moderate oven 185°C (350°F) until cheese melts or heat under a hot grill.

Serve on warm plates garnished with lemon and watercress.

BRAISED LAMB FILLETS

2 lamb rib loin fillets
oil for brushing
20 g butter
1 clove garlic, bruised
sprigs of rosemary
2 tablespoons white wine
salt and pepper

Garnish
lemon slices and
sprigs of rosemary

Brush lamb fillets in the piece with oil. Melt butter in pan and cook garlic lightly for 1 minute to flavour butter. Discard garlic.

Sear lamb fillets on the outside. Add rosemary and cook over moderate heat about 8 minutes turning the meat frequently. Remove and keep warm.

Add wine, salt and pepper to pan, heat until the sauce thickens slightly and set aside.

Slice lamb into round medallions (about 4 from from each fillet) and reheat in pan.

Arrange medallions on a platter and spoon sauce over. Serve garnished with lemon and sprigs of rosemary.

For serving, cooked green and white tagliatelle pasta may be served with Braised Lamb Fillets if desired.
Note: Use rack of lamb (6 chops in each) and remove bone to obtain larger medallions. Remove fat from other cuts if the butcher cannot supply rack of lamb.

Using a teaspoon, scoop the seeds out of tomato.

SNOW PEAS

12 snow peas (mangetout)
butter
salt and pepper

Snip stalks of peas with fingers. Plunge into boiling salted water. Cook until crisp yet tender. Drain and refresh in cold water. Cover and refrigerate if preparing ahead. Reheat in butter, salt and pepper just before serving.

TOMATOES PERSILLES

2 ripe tomatoes
1 tablespoon pine nuts
½ tablespoon oil
10 g butter
⅓ cup chopped parsley
1 clove garlic, crushed
salt and pepper

Halve and seed tomatoes. Sprinkle with salt. Drain upside down on absorbent paper.

Cook pine nuts in olive oil until slightly coloured and drain.

Melt butter and gently cook parsley and garlic. Season with salt and pepper.

Brush outside skin of tomatoes with oil and place in ovenproof dish. Spoon mixture into tomatoes and top with pine nuts. ☐

Heat through in moderate oven 180°C (350°F) until just tender.

PEACH ICE CREAM WITH FRESH PEACHES

3 large peaches
1½ cups cream
1 tablespoon Grand Marnier
½ cup sugar
¼ cup sugar syrup
1 tablespoon chopped pistachio nuts

Pour boiling water over 1 peach in a bowl. Stand 1 minute, drain, plunge into cold water then remove skin and stone the fruit. Puree to make ½ cup.

Combine puree with cream, 2 teaspoons Grand Marnier and sugar in food processor and blend until smooth and the sugar is dissolved. Pour into the container of an ice cream hand churn or into a freezer tray. Churn or freeze until of ice cream consistency. If a freezer tray is used, beat lightly halfway through freezing. Place freezer wrap over trays to prevent ice crystals forming.

If a churn is used, remove from churn and store in a covered container in the freezer until required. Scoop into ice cream balls and place on a metal slide covered with plastic wrap. □

Just before serving, peel the remaining peaches (as described previously) and cut each into 8 slices. Place in a bowl and baste with 2 tablespoons of sugar syrup and the remaining Grand Marnier. Cover to prevent fruit discolouring.

Place 2 scoops ice cream in individual bowls and arrange the fruit slices in a fan shape. Top with pistachio nuts and serve with madeleines (*see recipe*) or sponge finger biscuits.

MADELEINES

2 eggs
¼ cup caster sugar
½ cup sifted flour
60 g softened unsalted butter
2 teaspoons orange flower water
icing sugar

Prepare madeleine moulds. Oil well and turn upside down to drain.

Whisk eggs and sugar in mixer until thick and mousse-like. Fold in flour and softened butter. Add orange flower water. Fill prepared moulds with mixture.

Bake in preheated 190°C (375°F) oven for approximately 10 minutes. Cool. Remove carefully from pans. Dust with icing sugar.

Peach Ice Cream

DINNER FOR FOUR

A dinner that makes the most of fresh ingredients in their prime will put you on the road to successful entertaining. At first glance this menu may appear expensive — rest assured it is more dash than cash.

MENU

Two-Melon Summer Soup

Chicken Breasts au Poivre Vert
Sauteed Leeks
Pumpkin Timbales

Rum-marinated Mango Crepes

or

Coeur a la Creme

Served with Semillon

PREPARATION TIMETABLE

Prepare ahead and freeze: Crepes, Raspberry Sauce.

1 day ahead: Puree two melons for summer soup. Refrigerate in separate jugs.

Wash, trim and slice leeks. Refrigerate in a plastic bag. Prepare Coeur a la Creme and refrigerate or make crepes.

6 hours ahead: Prepare Chicken Breast au Poivre Vert up to stage of cooking. Place on a greased baking tray, cover and refrigerate. Chill beverages.

3 hours ahead: Prepare garnishes. Cover and refrigerate.

1 hour ahead: Prepare Pumpkin Timbales.

15 minutes ahead: Chill soup serving bowls. Make cream sauce to accompany Chicken Breasts Au Poivre Vert.

5 minutes ahead: Saute leeks.

Time for dinner: Pour melon purees into serving bowls. Spoon sauce over Chicken breasts. Unmould Pumpkin Timbales. Garnish dishes and serve. Just before conclusion of dinner, bake crepes.

Dessert: Fill crepes and dust with icing sugar to serve. Unmould Coeur a la Creme, dust with icing sugar, pour sauce around and arrange strawberries.

Clockwise from left: Chicken Breast au Poivre Vert with Sauteed Leeks and Pumpkin Timbales, Two Melon Summer Soup, Coeur a la Creme

TWO-MELON SUMMER SOUP

1 × 750 g rock melon (cantaloupe)
2 tablespoons fresh lemon juice
1 × 1 kg ripe honeydew melon
3 tablespoons fresh lime juice
2 teaspoons finely chopped fresh mint
mint sprigs for garnish
sour cream to serve if required

Cut the rock melon in half, scoop out the seeds and discard. Scoop out flesh and puree with the lemon juice in a food processor until smooth. Chill in a covered bowl for at least 12 hours.

Puree the honeydew melon with lime juice and mint until smooth and chill separately in a covered bowl for 12 hours. □

To serve, put the purees into separate jugs and pour at the same time but from separate sides into chilled serving bowls. The soup should stay in separate colours. Garnish with mint sprigs.
Note: This soup looks beautiful served in glass bowls.

CHICKEN BREAST AU POIVRE VERT

4 whole chicken breast fillets
3 tablespoons coarsely chopped pistachio nuts
4 slices German cream pepper cheese
salt and pepper
1 tablespoon lemon juice
30 g butter
3 slices cooked smoked ham, cut into fine strips, 5 cm long and 5 mm wide
2 tablespoons canned green peppercorns, rinsed, drained and loose skins discarded
¾ cup thickened cream (double cream)
1 teaspoon cornflour
2 tablespoons sour cream

Chicken Breast au Poivre Vert with Sauteed Leeks and Pumpkin Timbales

Open chicken breasts and flatten a little with a meat mallet. Place ½ tablespoon pistachio nuts along one section of each breast. Place slice of cheese on top and fold fillet over to encase stuffing. Shape breast and secure with toothpicks. □

Place in a greased baking dish and sprinkle with lemon juice, salt and pepper. Dot with half the butter, cover with aluminium foil and bake at 110°C (225°F) 15–20 minutes. Turn oven off.

Drain cooking juices from chicken into a saucepan. Replace aluminium foil over chicken and return to oven with door ajar to keep warm.

Combine ham and peppercorns and heat gently in a pan with remaining butter. Remove from pan.

Reduce cooking juices in pan to 1 tablespoon and strain. Mix cornflour with thickened cream and blend into cooking juices.

Cook sauce over moderate heat (without boiling) until thickened, add ham and peppercorns. Blend in sour cream. Spoon sauce over chicken breasts and serve.

Two-Melon Summer Soup. Pour the 2 soups from 2 jugs held on opposite sides of the bowl.

SAUTEED LEEKS

4 leeks, trimmed and washed
80 g butter

Cut the leeks into 5 cm × 5 mm wide strips and cook in butter over low heat until leeks are transparent and tender.

PUMPKIN TIMBALES

2 cups of pureed steamed pumpkin, dry, not moist
20 g butter, melted
4 eggs, beaten
1½ cups cream
½ teaspoon nutmeg
½ teaspoon cinnamon
salt and freshly ground black pepper
Italian parsley for garnish

Butter 6 souffle dishes or moulds. Combine pumpkin with butter, eggs, cream, nutmeg, cinnamon and pepper and blend well. Taste to correct seasoning.

Pour mixture into greased moulds. Place moulds into a baking dish and pour in enough boiling water to reach half way up the sides of the moulds. Cover with buttered greaseproof paper. Cook in a preheated oven at 200°C (400°F) 25–30 minutes until set.

Allow to rest 5 minutes before unmoulding. Garnish each with Italian parsley.

RUM-MARINATED MANGO CREPES

12 crepes (see recipe for Crepes Ninette)
2 ripe mangoes
2 tablespoons fresh lemon juice
½ tablespoon sugar
2 tablespoons rum (Lemon Heart)
90 g butter, melted
icing sugar, for dusting

Crepes may be prepared beforehand and stored in refrigerator (for up to 3 days) or freezer, in stacks of 6, with freezer wrap in between.

Peel mangoes and cut into pieces. Mix in a bowl with lemon juice, sugar and rum. Cover.

Fold crepes into quarters, arrange on baking tray, brush with butter and bake 10 minutes at 200°C (400°F).

Fill crepes with rum-marinated mango mixture between folds. Dust tops with icing sugar.

COEUR A LA CREME

375 g cream-style cottage cheese
250 g cream cheese
1 tablespoon icing sugar, sifted
¼ cup thickened cream (double cream), whipped
1 punnet raspberries or 250 g frozen, thawed
1 punnet fresh strawberries, for garnish

Cream together the 2 cheeses and fold in icing sugar and whipped cream. Line 6 Coeur a la Creme moulds with muslin and stand on a small tray. Spoon cheese mixture into moulds, smooth top and refrigerate overnight.

Unmould onto 6 dessert plates and remove muslin. Sift icing sugar over the top.

To make raspberry sauce, blend raspberries in processor. Sweeten to taste with icing sugar if desired. Spoon sauce around each Coeur a la Creme, placing strawberries to one side.

Note: Coeur a la Creme moulds are white, heart-shaped moulds available from cookware and department stores in the gourmet cookware section. Small ramekin moulds may be used as a substitute.

Coeur a la Creme

GOURMET DINNER FOR SIX

In the normal daily routine of eating out of necessity one can miss the opportunities to use cookery skills to their fullest. Presenting a gourmet menu for six may not be the first step for the commonsense cookery set but with careful planning following our easy recipes most cooks will impress their guests with the following menu.

MENU

Scallops and Asparagus Bouchee

Quail with Wild Rice
Pommes Noisettes
Baby Green and Yellow Squash
Warm Goat Cheese and Walnut Salad

Chestnut Bavarois

Served with Carbernet Sauvignon

PREPARATION TIMETABLE

Prepare ahead and freeze: Wholemeal Walnut Bread.
1 day ahead: Prepare bouchee cases (if home-made). Prepare quail stuffing. Cover and refrigerate. Prepare ingredients for Mirepoix.

Blanch yellow and green squash. Refrigerate in a plastic bag. Prepare and bake Walnut Bread. Store in an airtight container. Make Chestnut Bavoise. Refrigerate overnight.
6 hours ahead: Prepare Scallop and Asparagus filling for bouchee cases. Do not add scallops and mushrooms. Cover and refrigerate until ready to reheat. Prepare and stuff quail. Cook Mirepoix. Arrange quail in a baking dish, cover and refrigerate until time to roast. Chill beverages.
3 hours ahead: Soak juniper berries for sauce to serve with quail. Scoop out potato balls for Pommes Noisettes. Soak in cold water. Prepare garnishes. Whip cream and crystallise roses for Chestnut Bavoise.

1 hour ahead: Prepare salad greens and dressing. Prepare goat's cheese, place on baking sheet, cover and refrigerate until cooking time.
30 minutes ahead: Bake quail. Keep warm in a low oven. Prepare sauce to serve with quail. Cook, then fry potatoes for Pommes Noisettes. Keep warm in low oven.
15 minutes ahead: Heat bouchee cases. Cook yellow and green Baby Squash. Warm Walnut Bread in oven, if desired.
5 minutes ahead: Heat filling for bouchee cases. Stir in scallops and mushrooms. Reheat sauce to serve with quail. Cook goat's cheese.
Time for dinner: Fill bouchee cases with scallop mixture. Spoon sauce over Quail. Toss salad with dressing. Garnish all dishes and serve.
Dessert: Invert Chestnut Bavarois onto serving platter. Decorate with whipped cream and crystallised roses.

Clockwise from the front: Quail with Wild Rice , Warm Goat Cheese and Walnut Salad, Baby Green and Yellow Squash

SCALLOP AND ASPARAGUS BOUCHEE

30 g butter
12 button mushrooms, wiped, trimmed
  and sliced
2 tablespoons finely chopped shallots
¾ cup dry vermouth or dry white wine
4 scallops, rinsed and deveined
¾ cup fish stock
¾ cup cream
10 g butter blended with 2 teaspoons
  flour
12 asparagus spears, trimmed
1 tablespoon lemon juice
salt and pepper to taste
6 bouchee cases or 10 cm × 5 cm
  cooked puff pastry cases made from
  commerical puff pastry
sprigs of watercress and lemon slices,
  to garnish

Melt butter in a saucepan. Add mushrooms and gently cook until tender. Remove and set aside.

Cook shallots over a low heat until tender. Add the wine and slowly simmer. Add scallops and simmer 1–2 minutes. Remove and cover.

Simmer fish stock in pan and until reduced by ⅓. Add the cream and continue simmering until reduced slightly. Add blended flour and butter stirring until smooth and thickened.

Meanwhile, cook asparagus in boiling water until just becoming tender. Refresh under cold water, then drain. Cut tips from asparagus and set aside for garnish. Puree the stalks with lemon juice and seasoning to taste. Add asparagus puree to cream sauce together with mushrooms and scallops. Heat through without boiling.

Heat pastry cases at 180°C (350°F) for 10 minutes. Place on serving plates, fill with scallop mixture, arrange asparagus spears on top and garnish with watercress and a slice of lemon.

QUAIL WITH WILD RICE

9 quail, 1½ quail per serve

Stuffing
20 g butter
2 shallots, finely chopped
liver and heart of quail, diced
1½ cups wild rice, cooked
1 large red apple, cored and diced
2 tablespoons cream
1 egg yolk
salt and pepper to taste
pinch lemon thyme

Mirepoix
20 g butter
2 shallots, chopped
1 small carrot diced
1 small stick celery diced

Sauce
8 juniper berries marinated 2–3 hours in
  3 tablespoons Madeira
1½ cups chicken stock

Melt butter in a pan to make stuffing, add shallots and cook until softened. Add the liver and heart of quail and cook 5 minutes. Mix in the cooked wild rice and diced apple. Bind all ingredients together with cream and egg yolk and season to taste.

For the *Mirepoix*, melt butter, add vegetables and cook until tender. Spoon into the base of an ovenproof dish.

With quails on their backs and starting at the tail end, make an incision along breast. Carefully remove all small bones from breast and back sections, leaving the legs intact. □

Spoon stuffing into cavity then stitch incision with cotton. Arrange quails in the ovenproof dish in one layer. Roast at 200°C (400°F) 15–20 minutes basting frequently. Lift from dish, remove stitches and keep quails warm.

Discard vegetables but pour pan juices into a small saucepan. Add juniper berry mixture and chicken stock. Deglaze pan over medium heat, bring sauce to boil and reduce. Season. Strain. Spoon the sauce over the quail before serving.

Quail with Wild Rice and Baby Green and Yellow Squash

Scallop and Asparagus Bouchee

Using a melon baller, scoop peeled potatoes into balls. Set aside covered with water before using for Pommes Noisettes.

POMMES NOISETTES

1 kg potatoes, peeled
100 g butter
salt and pepper

Using a melon baller, scoop the potatoes into balls. Place in a bowl of cold water adding a pinch of salt. Cover and set aside 1 hour. Drain.

Bring a large saucepan of water to the boil. Add the potatoes and cook 3 minutes. Drain and dry thoroughly patting gently with absorbent paper.

Melt butter in a large frying pan. When foaming, add potatoes and cook, turning frequently, until golden-brown in colour. Season with salt and pepper and serve immediately.
Note: Use old potatoes for this recipe as they contain less starch and result in a crisper, brown noisette.

BABY GREEN AND YELLOW SQUASH

1 kg of mixed green and yellow squash
60 g butter
1 tablespoon orange juice
orange peel cut into fine threads, blanched, for garnish

Wash and trim squash. Cook in boiling salted water until crisp and tender. Drain and refresh under cold water and drain again.

Just before serving, melt butter, add squash and orange juice and heat through. Garnish with orange threads and serve.
Note: If squash are medium-sized, cut into vertical slices.

WARM GOAT CHEESE AND WALNUT SALAD

Walnut Dressing
1 tablespoon sherry vinegar
½ teaspoon dry mustard
salt and pepper to taste
pinch sugar
3 tablespoons safflower oil
1 tablespoon walnut oil

Salad
200 g goats cheese
⅓ cup finely chopped walnuts
curly endive
radicchio, washed, dried and torn into bite-sized pieces
2 shallots, chopped finely
½ teaspoon chopped chervil

For serving
Walnut Bread (see recipe)

Prepare dressing by combining all ingredients and shaking in glass jar until blended. Taste and adjust flavour if necessary.

Sprinkle nuts over cheese and press into surface. Place on a baking sheet and cook 3 minutes in oven at 200°C (400°F).

Combine salad greens. Toss with dressing in serving bowl.

Serve warm cheese with salad greens and Walnut Bread.

WALNUT BREAD

2 cups wholemeal flour
1 cup plain flour
1 cup rye flour
½ cup chopped walnuts
1 teaspoon salt
15 g fresh yeast or 7 g dry yeast
2 teaspoons golden syrup
1¼ cups warm water

Glaze
1 egg yolk
½ teaspoon golden syrup
water

Combine flours, walnuts and salt in a bowl. Cream yeast with syrup and add water in a bowl. Stand in a warm place 10 minutes to prepare yeast sponge.

Make a well in flour, add yeast mixture and mix into a dough. Knead until smooth and elastic.

Place in a greased bowl, cover and prove in a warm place until double in bulk, about ¾–1 hour. Punch down. Shape into a loaf. Place in a greased loaf tin. Cover and allow to rise to top of tin. Brush with glaze.

Bake in preheated oven for 10 minutes at 220°C (425°F). Reduce heat to 200°C (400°F) and bake for 30 minutes until cooked and brown. Bread may be prepared ahead and frozen. Bring to room temperature to serve.

To crystallise flowers, brush lightly with egg white then dip in sugar to coat each petal. Set aside to dry.

CHESTNUT BAVAROIS

8 egg yolks
1 cup sugar
2 cups milk
2 teaspoons vanilla
2 tablespoons gelatine softened in
   ½ cup cold water
½ cup chestnut puree
600 mL thickened cream (double
   cream), chilled
2 tablespoons dark rum

Decoration
300 mL cream, whipped
fresh baby roses, crystallised

Rinse a 1.5-litre mould with water. Place in freezer to chill thoroughly.

Combine egg yolks with sugar and beat 10 minutes or until the mixture is thick and a pale lemon colour. Scald the milk and gradually add to the mixture, gently stirring. Transfer to the top half of a double boiler and thicken over simmering water until the custard coats the back of a metal spoon. Remove from the heat, cool slightly adding the softened gelatine, stir until dissolved.

Beat the chestnut puree with a little of the custard to form a smooth consistency. Stir into the remaining custard. Cool by standing in a basin of iced water (do not allow to set).

Beat cream only until soft peaks form, adding the rum. Both the custard and the cream should be of the same consistency. Fold together. Pour the mixture into the mould and refrigerate for several hours until firm to the touch.

Loosen Bavarois from around the sides of the mould, invert onto a serving platter. ☐ Pipe whipped cream around the base of the Bavarois and decorate with the crystallised roses.

Note: Chestnut Bavarois is a rich, mousse-like dessert set in a mould. Decorate with baby roses. Chestnut puree may be found at your supermarket and is sold in cans. In hot weather, add an extra tablespoon of gelatine.

To crystallise roses
fresh baby roses, rinsed
1 egg white, lightly beaten
1 cup caster sugar

Lightly paint the egg white onto the roses with a small paint brush. Dip the roses into the sugar, coating each petal. Shake off any excess. Arrange on greaseproof paper and set aside for several hours to dry.

Chestnut Bavarois

FORMAL DINNER FOR EIGHT

A formal dinner for eight is entertaining in the most stylish sense. Create an elegant approach to the evening by sending out written invitations — your guests will find it hard to resist. Set the table with crisp linen, glasses and cutlery all sparkling and pull out all the stops to make it a memorable occasion.

MENU

Stuffed Mushrooms

Celery Cream Soup

Roast Beef with Peppercorn Crust
Roast Pumpkin
Spinach Cream Mould
Citrus Salad

Pear Tart with Frangipani Cream

Served with Shiraz

Roast Beef with Peppercorn Crust

PREPARATION TIMETABLE

1 day ahead: Prepare filling for Stuffed Mushrooms. Refrigerate in a covered container. Chop celery and onions for soup. Refrigerate in a plastic bag. Prepare seasoning for Spiced Beef Roll. Cover and refrigerate. Cook pears in sugar syrup. Cool, place on absorbent paper on a flat tray. Cover with plastic wrap and refrigerate. Prepare frangipani cream. Cover and refrigerate.

6 hours ahead: Prepare Espagnole Sauce. Cover with plastic wrap to prevent skin forming and refrigerate. Prepare, roll up and tie Spiced Beef Roll, place in baking dish, cover and refrigerate. Prepare Spinach Cream mixture and refrigerate in a covered jug. Prepare flan shell for Pear Tart, bake blind and allow to cool.

3 hours ahead: Prepare Celery Cream Soup. Cover and refrigerate until ready to heat and serve. Cut pumpkin, ready for roasting. Cover and refrigerate. Assemble and bake Pear Tart. Brush with Apricot glaze when cooked. Whip cream to serve with dessert.

2 hours ahead: Complete preparation of Spiced Beef Roll and bake. Prepare garnishes.

1 hour ahead: Bake pumpkin. Prepare salad and dressing. Cover and refrigerate.

30 minutes ahead: Arrange mushroom caps on a greased baking dish. Spoon filling into caps. Cover and refrigerate until ready to bake. Carve Spiced Beef Roll. Keep warm in oven, covered with aluminium foil. Bake Spinach Cream Mould. Prepare Mornay Sauce (if serving). Cover and reheat just before serving. Open red wine if serving.

15 minutes ahead: Bake Stuffed Mushrooms. Prepare ham and lettuce for serving with Stuffed Mushrooms. Heat Celery Cream Soup. Reheat Espagnole Sauce.

Time for dinner: Arrange Stuffed Mushroom and Spiced Beef Roll slices on serving platters. Invert Spinach Cream Mould onto serving plates. Toss salad with dressing. Garnish dishes and serve.

Dessert: Carefully remove Pear Tart from flan tin. Serve sliced, on a platter or on individual plates.

Citrus Salad
Celery Cream Soup
Roast Beef with Peppercorn Crust

STUFFED MUSHROOMS

16 mushroom caps

Filling
½ cup fresh white breadcrumbs
½ cup finely grated Parmesan cheese
1 cup chopped ham
2 tablespoons capers, finely chopped
½ cup grated Swiss cheese
1 clove garlic, crushed
¼ cup finely chopped parsley
salt and freshly ground black pepper
lemon juice
2 tablespoons olive oil

For serving
8 slices smoked ham
6 lettuce leaves
1 tablespoon lemon juice

Carefully remove stalks from mushrooms. Chop stalks and mix chopped stalks with filling ingredients except for seasoning, lemon juice and oil.

Arrange mushroom caps in a buttered ovenproof dish. Season with a sprinkle of salt and pepper and a squeeze of lemon juice. Spoon filling evenly into caps, shaping a little. Sprinkle with olive oil and bake for 8 minutes at 200°C (400°F).

Cut ham into circles with a scone cutter. Heat lettuce with lemon juice very gently in a covered saucepan until it has wilted.

Place a ham circle under each mushroom cap and serve on the bed of lettuce.

CELERY CREAM SOUP

60 g butter
3 onions, chopped
1 bunch celery, chopped
1.5 litres beef stock
300 mL thickened cream (double cream)
salt and pepper
celery seeds, for garnish

Cook onions in butter until transparent. Stir in beef stock and simmer 45 minutes. Blend until smooth in food processor. This may be done in several batches. Add cream and season with salt and pepper to taste.

Reheat (without boiling) and sprinkle lightly with celery seeds to serve.

ROAST BEEF WITH PEPPERCORN CRUST

3 kg beef sirloin
2 teaspoons black peppercorns, coarsely ground
1 teaspoon dried green peppercorns
½ teaspoon white peppercorns, coarsely ground
4 whole allspice, coarsely ground
½ teaspoon dried thyme
½ teaspoon coarse salt
1 clove garlic, crushed

Sauce
reserved pan juices from roast
½ cup red wine
2 cups beef stock or broth
½ cup Madeira
1 tablespoon cornflour
2 tablespoons Dijon mustard

In a bowl, combine peppercorns and herbs. Rub into the surface of the meat. Place in a roasting pan fat side up and bake at 250°C (475°F) for 30 minutes. Reduce heat to 175°C (350°F) and roast meat for approximately 2 hours.

It should be medium rare when done. Leave oven door ajar with oven off and allow to stand 20 minutes before carving. Reserve the pan juices for making the sauce.

Skim the fat from the pan juices. Add red wine to the pan over a moderate heat. Cook until the liquid has reduced by ½ then transfer to a saucepan. Add broth, ¼ cup Madeira and boil 5 minutes.

Mix cornflour with the remaining Madeira and add whisk into sauce. Bring to the boil and cook until thickened to pouring sauce consistency. Season and serve.

ROAST PUMPKIN

1 kg pumpkin, seeds removed
2 tablespoons beef dripping or oil
2 tablespoons corn syrup
toasted pumpkin seeds, for serving

Cut the pumpkin into large serve-size wedges. Arrange on a baking tray and brush with the beef dripping or oil. Bake at the same time as the meat for 35–40 minutes. In the final 10 minutes brush pumpkin with corn syrup to glaze. Serve with toasted pumpkin seeds.

SPINACH CREAM MOULD

500 g frozen spinach, thawed
1 cup fine white dry breadcrumbs, soaked in ½ cup hot milk
1 tablespoon sour cream
2 eggs
salt and pepper
nutmeg

Garnish
2 bacon rashers, chopped and grilled until crisp
8 mushroom caps, cooked

Drain spinach and press out excess liquid. Add soaked crumbs, sour cream, and beaten egg. Season well. Spoon into 8 buttered and crumbed ovenproof moulds or a 5-cup mould. Fill to top and cover with buttered paper.

Stand moulds in a roasting pan with sufficient water to come halfway up the sides. Bake at 180°C (350°F) for 30 minutes or until firm. Remove from hot water and leave 2–3 minutes to set. Unmould and garnish with mushrooms and bacon.
Note: Serve with a mornay sauce if desired.

Spinach Cream Mould

CITRUS SALAD

Dressing
2 cloves garlic
juice of 1 lemon
1 tablespoon white wine vinegar
pinch curry powder
salt
freshly ground pepper
1 tablespoon olive or vegetable oil
1 teaspoon walnut oil
1 lettuce, washed and dried
4 oranges, peeled and segmented
16 walnuts
1½ cups alfalfa
chopped parsley

Combine crushed garlic, lemon juice, wine vinegar, curry powder, salt, pepper, olive or vegetable oil and walnut oil in a jar and shake well.

Toss lettuce in a bowl with orange segments and walnuts and alfalfa. Pour over dressing before serving. Taste for seasoning and sprinkle with parsley.

PEAR TART WITH FRANGIPANI CREAM

1 quantity of pate sucree or 2 sheets
    ready-rolled shortcrust pastry
4 pears, peeled and cored, cut into
    halves

Syrup
2 cups water
1 cup sugar
strip of lemon rind

Frangipani Cream
120 g unsalted butter
½ cup sugar
2 large eggs, beaten
1 cup blanched almonds, ground
1 tablespoon flour
almond liqueur or kirsch or almond
    essence

Glaze
¾ cup apricot jam, warmed and sieved

Line base and sides of a 25 cm metal flan tin with pate sucree or ready-rolled pastry. Trim edges and bake blind at 200°C (400°F) for 10 minutes. Cool before filling.

Cook pears in the water, sugar and lemon rind, until just tender. Cool in syrup then drain on paper towels.

Cream butter and sugar together and add eggs a little at a time, beating well.

Pear Tart with Frangipani Cream

Combine almonds, flour, kirsch or almond essence together and add.

Spoon ½ the Frangipani Cream over pastry base. Arrange pear halves on this, cut side facing down. Spread the remaining cream mixture around and over the pears. Bake at 175°C (350°F) for 40 minutes, until cream is set and golden-brown. Brush with apricot glaze.

Serve with whipped cream very lightly flavoured with almond liqueur or cinnamon.

FOREIGN AFFAIRS

A truly mixed up section this, with menus from Greece, Italy, France, India, Indonesia and China, yet such is the fellowship of the cuisines of the world that the feeling is one of a serendipitous balance of flavours and textures. Over the past two decades, many cooks have moved towards more sophisticated foreign recipes, away from the mastered basics. Meeting the appetite for the internationally diverse, this collection of recipes ranges from Moussaka to Pizzaiola Mussels — from Lamb Curry to Spicy Pork Sate and Peanut Sauce.

In many cases, foreign food is conversation food, to be lingered over, savoured and discussed. This is also the time to bring out your wonderful Mediterranean pottery, French country platters bronze Asian bowls and oriental porcelain. Creating a transplanted sliver of the country whose cuisine you are serving, adds immeasurably to the enjoyment of the occasion. Fortunately, these days, you don't have to actually go to every far-flung place. Department stores and cookware shops can provide you with European choices and decorations, Asian emporiums and local Chinatowns offer a wide range of oriental serving ware.

Avoid being rigid when you plan. Things do not have to be all Greek, French, Italian or Chinese. Try to visualise what food will look like as separate dishes and as part of a meal. Go for strong colours in some of the selections, such as hors d'oeuvres, pasta, desserts and so on, ending up with an international menu entente cordiale.

Even the most esoteric ingredients are becoming easier to find; food shops vie with each other to stock the most way-out ingredients. When planning a Greek meal, go to a Greek delicatessen. The olives, vine leaves and tarama will taste more authentic than similar homogenised supermarket items. The same thinking should be applied to every other ethnic cuisine as well — stores catering to their own ethnic communities have to rival memories of "back home".

It's also a good idea to match a particular country's food with its homegrown wines. French and Italian wines are widely available in all price categories. Greek wines can be a problem, as not everyone appreciates the mouth-puckering taste of retsina. If retsina's not your flavour, choose a full-bodied red wine. Asian food in general defies wine choices, although Cantonese cooking accommodates light, fruity white wines. Indian and Indonesian food goes best with beer or mineral water.

Clockwise from left: Spicy Pork Sate, Cucumbers in Yoghurt, Fried Noodles with Chicken and Vegetables, Gado-Gado

INDONESIAN DISHES FOR SIX

The dishes in this menu are probably familiar to all. Fried noodles with Chicken and Vegetables makes a mouth-watering starter, while Gado-Gado (Indonesian Salad), Nasi (white rice), Spicy Pork Sate with Peanut Sauce, and Cucumbers in Yoghurt create a table with a range of flavours for the main course. A fresh fruit platter is the perfect finale.

MENU

Fried Noodles with Chicken and Vegetables

Gado-Gado
Spicy Pork Sate and Peanut Sauce
Nasi
Cucumbers in Yoghurt

Fruit Platter

Served with Riesling, Light Ale or Mineral Water

PREPARATION TIMETABLE

1 day ahead: Prepare and blanch vegetables for Gado-Gado. Refrigerate in plastic bags. Prepare chicken fillets, prawns and vegetables for Fried Noodles with Chicken and Vegetables. Refrigerate in covered containers until ready to cook.

6 hours ahead: Make Peanut Sauce and refrigerate. Prepare Spicy Pork Sate marinade. Marinate pork cubes in refrigerator. Turn over occasionally. Prepare Nasi. Cool, cover and refrigerate until ready to reheat. Chill white wine.

3 hours ahead: Arrange Gado-Gado on serving platter. Cover with plastic wrap and chill until ready to serve. Prepare cucumbers and boil eggs for Cucumbers in Yoghurt. Prepare garnishes. Soak wooden kebab skewers in cold water. Prepare fruit for Fruit Platter. Chill until ready to arrange on a platter.

1 hour ahead: Combine stock, cornflour and soy sauce for Fried Noodles with Chicken and Vegetables. Set aside. Thread pork onto skewers. Place on a tray, cover and refrigerate until ready to grill. Complete preparation of Cucumbers in Yoghurt. Refrigerate in a covered bowl.

30 minutes ahead: Deep-fry noodles. Set aside on individual plates until ready to top with Chicken and Vegetables. Grill pork kebabs. Keep warm in oven. Reheat Nasi in oven.

15 minutes ahead: Stir fry Chicken and Vegetables. Heat serving dish for Spicy Pork Sate. Heat Spicy Pork Sate marinade. Thin out Peanut Sauce if necessary. Pour Peanut Sauce over Gado-Gado. Break brown bread into serving pieces. Arrange in a basket.

Time for dinner: Spoon Chicken and Vegetables over Fried Noodles. Arrange on serving plate with Peanut Sauce. Fluff up Nasi with a fork. Garnish dishes and serve.

Dessert: Arrange fruit decoratively on serving platter.

Gado-Gado with Peanut Sauce

Fried Noodles with Chicken and Vegetables

FRIED NOODLES WITH CHICKEN AND VEGETABLES

250 g fresh rice noodles, divided into 6
   portions
oil for deep frying
2 chicken fillets, cut into small pieces
100 g shelled cooked prawns, deveined
1 clove garlic, crushed
salt and pepper
1 piece bamboo shoot, shredded
6 dried mushrooms, soaked for 1 hour
   and sliced
1 cup mixed vegetables, carrots, red
   and green capsicum (pepper), green
   beans, shallots, cut into matchstick
   lengths
½ cup chicken stock
½ teaspoon cornflour
1 tablespoon soy sauce

Deep-fry each portion of noodles in hot
oil until golden brown and drain on
kitchen paper. ☐

Heat wok, add 1 tablespoon oil and
stir-fry chicken and prawns with garlic
5–10 minutes. Season with salt and
pepper. Add bamboo shoots, mushrooms and vegetables and fry a further
3–4 minutes.

Combine stock, cornflour and soy
sauce and pour over chicken and vegetables. Bring to the boil and simmer 2
minutes until mixture has thickened.

To serve, place one portion of fried
noodles on each plate and spoon
chicken mixture on top. Serve
immediately.

GADO-GADO

2 large carrots, sliced thinly
200 g green beans, strung
200 g bean sprouts
1 cup shredded cabbage
1 large onion, chopped
1 cucumber, sliced thinly
3 eggs, hard-boiled
2 tablespoons chopped shallots, to
   garnish

Sauce
1 cup roasted peanuts, unsalted
3 cloves garlic, peeled
½ teaspoon salt
⅓ cup sugar
3 tablespoons lemon juice or vinegar

Blanch carrots in boiling salted water
for 2 minutes and drain. Slice beans diagonally, blanch 2 minutes and drain.
Blanch bean sprouts, cabbage and
onion for 1 minute and drain.

Toss vegetables together and arrange on a platter with cucumber and
sliced eggs. Set aside,

Combine all sauce ingredients and
blend or process until mixture is thick
and smooth.

Drizzle sauce over vegetables and
garnish with shallots.

SPICY PORK SATE AND PEANUT SAUCE

500 g pork fillet

Marinade
¼ cup soy sauce
¼ cup dry sherry
1 clove garlic, crushed
1 thin slice fresh root ginger, finely
    chopped
1 teaspoon curry powder
2 tablespoons oil

Peanut Sauce
⅔ cup fresh peanuts, finely chopped
1 teaspoon honey
few drops chilli sauce
1 teaspoon tomato sauce
1 teaspoon lemon juice
¼ cup peanut butter
1 teaspoon cornflour

Cut pork into 3 cm cubes. Mix together soy sauce, sherry, garlic, ginger, curry powder and oil, and marinate pork pieces for 3 hours, basting from time to time. ☐

Thread meat on kebab skewers. Grill kebabs, turning frequently, until browned on all sides.

Meanwhile, heat marinade with sauce ingredients except cornflour. Thicken if required with cornflour mixed with a little water, stirring to blend to a smooth sauce.

On a heated serving dish, arrange sates on a bed of rice. Spoon Peanut Sauce over sates or serve sauce separately.

NASI

2 cups long-grain rice, washed and
    drained
2½ cups water
2 teaspoons salt

Bring water and salt to boil. Add rice gradually and return to boil, stirring continuously. Reduce heat to low, cover pan and cook rice until tender and all liquid has been absorbed. Serve hot.

CUCUMBERS IN YOGHURT

3 cucumbers, peeled and cubed
3 cups thick, natural yoghurt
2 cloves garlic, crushed
½ teaspoon salt
cracked black pepper
1 tablespoon melted butter
1 tablespoon oil
1 tablespoon wine vinegar
2 tablespoons chopped fresh dill
2 tablespoons chopped parsley
½ cup walnuts, chopped
2 hard-boiled eggs, shelled and
    crumbled

Mix ingredients together in a bowl and chill 1 hour. Serve with coarse brown bread.

FRUIT PLATTER

½ pineapple, cut into pieces
1 ripe mango, cut into pieces
2 bananas, cut into pieces and
    sprinkled with lemon juice
1 coconut, broken into pieces (drain
    milk)
250 g fresh lychees
1 grapefruit, segmented
1 tablespoon sugar
mint leaves for garnish

Arrange fruit decoratively on a platter, and sprinkle lightly with 1 tablespoon sugar. Garnish with mint leaves and serve chilled.

Serving suggestion: Line platter within banana leaves and decorate with frangipani.

Tropical Fruit Platter

MIDDLE-EASTERN MENU FOR EIGHT

Popular dishes from around the Mediterranean are perfect for low cost, relaxed entertaining. The following menu will easily satisfy eight guests. Palms, figs and citrus all add atmosphere as will the warm glow from candles and brass servingware. Seat your guests at a low table with scattered cushions — perfect for lounging and lingering over dishes such as Fried Fish with Tahina, Moussaka or Eggplant Pilaf.

MENU

Greek Appetiser Platter

Hummus
Fried Fish with Tahina

Moussaka
Pilaf with Eggplant
Beetroot Salad

Honey Puffs
Turkish Coffee

Served with Chablis

PREPARATION TIMETABLE

1 day ahead: Prepare Hummus. Cover and refrigerate. Prepare vegetables to serve with Hummus. Refrigerate in plastic bag. Prepare Moussaka up to cooking stage. Cover and refrigerate overnight.

6 hours ahead: Prepare and cook Pilaf with Eggplant (if serving cold). Cool, cover and chill in refrigerator. Prepare Honey Puff dough. Grind coffee beans for Turkish Coffee. Chill beverages.

3 hours ahead: Prepare and arrange Greek appetiser platter. Cover and refrigerate. Prepare Beetroot Salad. Cover and refrigerate. Fry Honey Puffs. Allow to cool, set aside in an airtight container.

1 hour ahead: Bake Moussaka. Prepare and cook Pilaf with Eggplant (if serving hot). Arrange raw vegetables and Hummus on a serving platter. Cover and refrigerate. Prepare garnishes.

30 minutes ahead: Cut fish fillets. Cover and refrigerate. Prepare Honey Puff syrup. Cool, cover and set aside until serving time.

15 minutes ahead: Warm bread in oven to accompany appetiser platter. Roll fish fillets in seasoned flour, dip in egg. Prepare Tahina. Cook fish.

Time for dinner: Cut Moussaka into squares. Garnish dishes and serve.

Dessert: Make Turkish Coffee. Coat Honey Puffs in syrup, sprinkle with cinnamon and serve.

Clockwise from left: Hummus, Moussaka, Pilaf with Eggplant, Beetroot Salad

GREEK APPETISER PLATTER

150 g green olives
150 g black Kalamata olives
1 teaspoon cracked coriander
1 clove garlic, crushed
1 tablespoon olive oil
2 tomatoes, quartered
1 soft-skinned cucumber, sliced thickly
200 g feta cheese, cut into 2 cm cubes
200 g kasseri cheese, cut into 1 cm and
    4 cm sticks (or other goat's milk
    cheese)
250 g cooked prawns, shelled
250 g pickled baby octopus
4 bread rolls, warmed and halved

Put olives into a bowl. Sprinkle with coriander, garlic and olive oil. Mix and set aside.

Arrange remaining ingredients, except the bread, on a large platter or prepare individual servings. Serve with the warmed bread and the bowl of green and black olives.

Note: The Greek Appetiser Platter consists of an assortment of light finger foods, served before dinner to whet the appetite. The platter is filled with your choice of raw, cooked and pickled vegetables, cheeses, fruits, bread, cold meats, sausages and seafood. As the Greeks say: "KALI OREXI!"

HUMMUS

500 g canned Garbanzo beans (chick
    peas), drained
2 cloves garlic, crushed
½ teaspoon ground cumin
½ teaspoon salt
½ cup olive
2 teaspoons sesame oil
¼ cup lemon juice
1 tablespoon chopped parsley

Pound chickpeas until smooth then stir in garlic, cumin and salt. Add tablespoons of oil and lemon juice alternately, blending well each time, until mixture forms smooth, thick paste. This dip can be made in a blender or food processor.

Transfer mixture to serving bowl, cover and chill well. Garnish with chopped parsley and serve with bread and a selection of raw vegetables.

Note: The flavour of this Lebanese dip improves with keeping. Prepare in advance and refrigerate in a covered container.

Fried Fish with Tahina

FRIED FISH WITH TAHINA

8 fish fillets, bream, ocean perch or
    flounder
1 cup flour, seasoned with salt and
    pepper
2 eggs, beaten
½ cup oil
2 cloves garlic, crushed
1 cup tahina
1 cup water
2 teaspoons lemon juice

Garnish
1 tablespoon chopped chives
1 lime or lemon, sliced thinly

Cut each fillet in half. Season fish pieces in flour and dip in beaten egg.

Heat oil and lightly saute garlic. Cook fish on both sides in hot oil until golden.

Combine tahina with water and lemon juice and pour over fish. Cook over low heat for further 5 minutes. Garnish with lemon or lime slices and chopped chives.

MOUSSAKA

5 large eggplants (aubergine), sliced
    and sprinkled with salt
3 tablespoons oil
60 g butter
1.5 kg minced lamb or beef
4 onions, chopped
2 teaspoons salt
freshly ground black pepper
½ teaspoon cinnamon
8 ripe tomatoes, peeled and chopped
½ cup chopped parsley
4–6 tablespoons water
1 cup breadcrumbs
1 cup grated Parmesan cheese
4 tablespoons grated tasty cheese

Sauce
80 g butter
4 tablespoons flour
1 litre milk
6 egg yolks, beaten

After 15 minutes rinse and drain eggplant slices.

Heat oil and fry eggplant slices until lightly browned on both sides. Remove and drain on absorbent paper.

Melt butter and brown meat. Add onions and fry until golden. Season with salt, pepper and cinnamon. Add tomatoes, parsley and water. Bring to boil and simmer 20–30 minutes.

Sprinkle half the breadcrumbs into a large buttered baking dish and layer meat, eggplant and half the cheeses. To make a smooth sauce, stir continuously. Melt butter, add flour and cook 1 minute. Remove from heat, add milk gradually and then bring to boil, stirring continuously. Simmer 3–5 minutes.

Beat 2 tablespoons of the hot sauce into the eggs then pour egg mixture back into remaining sauce, beating all the time. Season to taste, cover and keep warm. Pour white sauce over moussaka and sprinkle with remaining cheese and breadcrumbs. □

Bake at 180°C (350°F) for 1 hour, or until crust is crisp and brown. Cut into squares and serve hot.

PILAF WITH EGGPLANT

4 small eggplants (aubergine)
1 tablespoon salt
3 tablespoons olive oil
2 tomatoes, peeled, seeded and
    chopped
1 clove garlic, crushed
¼ teaspoon salt
freshly ground black pepper
1 cup Basmati or long grain rice
2 cups hot chicken stock

Cut the eggplants in half lengthways then into 1 cm thick slices. Sprinkle with salt and set aside for 15 minutes. Rinse and pat dry with paper towels.

Heat the olive oil in a large casserole and saute the eggplant slices until lightly browned on both sides. Add tomatoes and garlic and simmer over low heat 5 minutes, stirring occasionally. Add salt, pepper and rice and combine thoroughly. Pour in the hot stock and bring to the boil. Lower the heat, cover and simmer until the rice has absorbed all the liquid (about 25 minutes).

Place the casserole on a simmer pad over the lowest possible heat and cook 15 minutes more.

Serve hot or cold with a side dish of natural yoghurt.

BEETROOT SALAD

1½ tablespoons olive oil
1 tablespoon lemon juice
1¼ cups natural yoghurt
1 clove garlic, crushed
¼ teaspoon salt
⅓ teaspoon white pepper
250 g cooked beetroot, diced
2 tablespoons finely chopped parsley,
    to garnish

In a bowl, beat the olive oil and lemon juice with a wire whisk. Add the yoghurt, garlic, salt and pepper and stir until thoroughly blended. Fold in the diced beetroot and transfer to a serving bowl. Sprinkle with parsley and serve.
Note: Canned baby beets can be substituted if fresh beetroot not available.

HONEY PUFFS

5 cups flour, sifted
1 teaspoon salt
1 packet dry yeast
2 cups lukewarm water
oil for deep-frying

Syrup
1 cup honey
1½ cups sugar
1½ cups water
4 teaspoons lemon juice
4 teaspoons cinnamon to garnish

Sift flour and salt in bowl. Sprinkle yeast over water and stir. Combine yeast with flour and beat until dough is not sticky but smooth and elastic. Cover and set aside until dough has doubled in size.

Heat oil. Pinch off small pieces (approximately 1 tablespoon) of dough and drop into hot oil. Fry till crisp and golden. Drain puffs on absorbent paper.

Combine honey, sugar, water and lemon juice and bring to the boil, stirring until sugar dissolves. Allow to boil until mixture has thickened slightly.

Coat each puff in syrup and serve sprinkled with cinnamon.

TURKISH COFFEE

1½ teaspoons finely ground Turkish
    coffee per person
1½ teaspoons sugar per person
⅓ cup cold water per person

The coffee should be so finely ground it is almost pulverised. Place all ingredients in the pot and bring slowly to the boil. When foam rises, remove from heat and stir. Repeat this process twice. Do not stir the final time. Sprinkle with a little cold water to allow grounds to settle and serve in small coffee cups.
Note: If Turkish coffee beans are not available, try finely ground mocca beans as an alternative. Don't drink the sediment in the coffee cups.

Honey Puffs

AN ITALIAN MENU FOR TWO

For an evening with an Italian flavour, this light menu is perfect. The recipes require little in the way of preparation time or special culinary skills, but the dishes are in true Italian style served with vino and crusty Italian bread.

MENU

Pizzaiola Mussels

Veal Marsala
Vegetable Risotto

Peach and Champagne Sorbet

Served with Cabernet Shiraz

PREPARATION TIMETABLE

1 day ahead: Chop parsley, grate cheese, squeeze lemon ready to add other ingredients the next day. Refrigerate in covered containers.

Prepare and blanch vegetables for Vegetable Risotto. Refrigerate in a plastic bag.

Prepare Peach and Champagne Sorbet.

6 hours ahead: Scrub and soak mussels. Prepare tomato topping, cover and refrigerate. Flatten Veal Fillets. Cover with plastic wrap and refrigerate. Prepare asparagus. Refrigerate until ready to steam. Cook Arborio rice for Vegetable Risotto.

3 hours ahead: Complete preparation of Vegetable Risotto. Place into greased casserole, cover and refrigerate until cooking time. Open mussels and place on a flat ovenproof dish. Top with tomato mixture, sprinkle over parsley and cheese. Cover and refrigerate until ready to bake.

1 hour ahead: Prepare garnishes.

30 minutes ahead: Open red wine and allow to breathe.

15 minutes ahead: Bake Vegetable Risotto.

10 minutes ahead: Bake Pizzaiola Mussels. Steam asparagus. Fry Veal Fillets, make Marsala Sauce and saute mushrooms.

Time for dinner: Garnish dishes and serve immediately. Chill serving glasses for Peach and Champagne Sorbet.

Dessert: Spoon scoops of sorbet into each glass. Pour Champagne over and serve.

Clockwise from top right: Pizzaiola Mussels, Vegetable Risotto, Veal Marsala

Wash mussels well. Remove fibres from shell using a small sharp knife.

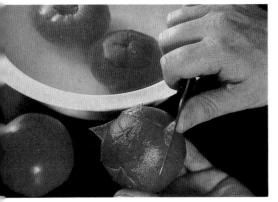

To peel tomato, remove stem end, cut a cross shape on the top and stand tomato in boiling water for 3 minutes. Starting at top of tomato, peel back skin.

PIZZAIOLA MUSSELS

14 mussels
1 tablespoon butter
1 onion chopped
1 clove garlic, crushed
2 tomatoes, peeled, seeded and
  chopped
1 bouquet garni
1 tablespoon lemon juice
salt and pepper
1 tablespoon finely chopped parsley
½ cup grated cheese

Scrub mussels thoroughly and soak in cold water for 20 minutes.

Heat butter in pan and gently cook onion and garlic until soft. Add tomatoes, bouquet garni, lemon juice and seasoning and cook for 5 minutes.

Open mussels with a sharp knife, starting at hinge and working round to join. Place opened mussels on a flat ovenproof dish and cover with tomato mixture. Sprinkle with parsley and grated cheese and bake in oven at 180°C (350°F) 8 minutes.

Serve immediately with crusty bread to soak up the sauce.

VEAL MARSALA

2 large veal escalopes
¼ cup flour
pinch paprika
pinch dried basil
pinch oregano
salt and pepper
1 tablespoon oil
60 g butter
½ cup Marsala
½ cup cream
1 tablespoon lemon juice
100 g button mushrooms, sliced
2 tablespoons parsley chopped

Flatten veal with meat mallet. Combine flour, spices, herbs, salt and pepper. Dip escalopes in seasoned flour and shake off excess. □

Heat oil and butter in large frying pan. When sizzling hot, add veal and fry 1½ minutes on each side or until golden. Remove from pan and keep warm.

Drain off excess butter and oil. Pour Marsala into pan and boil for 2 minutes. Stir in cream and lemon juice, and cook 1 minute, shaking pan.

Add mushrooms to sauce and simmer 2 minutes, stirring constantly.

Pour sauce over veal and sprinkle with parsley.

Pizzaiola Mussels

VEGETABLE RISOTTO

1 cup green peas, fresh or frozen
½ red capsicum (pepper), chopped
1 medium-sized kohlrabi
1 carrot, diced
1 parsnip, diced
8 mushrooms, sliced
2 tablespoons butter
½ cup grated cheddar cheese
2 tablespoons sour cream
1 tablespoon tomato juice
¾ cup cooked arborio rice
salt to taste

Preheat oven to 180°C (350°F). Blanch all vegetables separately in boiling salted water. Drain.

Mix butter with cheese, sour cream and tomato juice. Add rice, salt, vegetables and stir.

Place in a greased casserole, cover and bake 15 minutes.

PEACH AND CHAMPAGNE SORBET

⅔ cup caster sugar
500 g white peaches
juice of ½ lemon
1½ glasses champagne
sponge fingers, for serving

Place sugar in saucepan with ¼ cup water. Simmer, stirring to dissolve sugar. Set aside to cool.

Place peaches in sufficient boiling water to cover and simmer 1½ minutes. Peel, remove stones and cut flesh into chunks. Sprinkle with lemon juice, then puree.

Whisk peach puree and cooled syrup together. Pour mixture into freezer trays and freeze until firm, stirring occasionally with fork. □

Chill serving glasses. Immediately before serving place two scoops of Peach Sorbet in each glass and pour champagne over.

Serve with sponge fingers.

Peach and Champagne Sorbet

DINNER WITH A FRENCH ACCENT FOR SIX

The beauty of French cuisine is the perfect balance of fine ingredients and flavours. Together they create dishes that appeal to the palate and eye. If you enjoy entertaining with fine foods and wine, but run short on time, then this is the ideal menu for you. Most of the recipes from this menu may be prepared in advance keeping the dinner's atmosphere as relaxed as a sunny afternoon in the Loire Valley.

MENU

Quiche Lorraine

Noisettes au Poivre Vert
Courgettes au Beurre
Salade Nicoise

Crepes Ninette

Served with White Burgundy

PREPARATION TIMETABLE

Prepare ahead and freeze: Crepes.
1 day ahead: Blanch zucchinis. Cover and refrigerate until ready to reheat. Prepare and cook crepes. Place between squares of greaseproof paper. Cover with plastic wrap and refrigerate. Prepare crepe filling. Cover and refrigerate.
6 hours ahead: Prepare shortcrust pastry for Quiche Lorraines. Bake and cool. If serving cold, fill pastry cases with cream mixture and cook. Allow to cool, cover and refrigerate until serving time. If serving hot, cover flan cases and set aside. Chill white wine.
3 hours ahead: Prepare Salade Nicoise. Prepare salad dressing. Cover and refrigerate. Chop parsley and basil for zucchinis in butter. Prepare garnishes.

1 hour ahead: Trim and tie lamb fillets with string. Place on a flat tray. Cover and refrigerate until ready to cook.
30 minutes ahead: If serving Quiche Lorraine hot, fill pastry cases with cream mixture and cook. Fill crepes with apple mixture. Cover and refrigerate.
15 minutes ahead: Cook lamb fillets. Keep warm in a low oven. Prepare Green Peppercorn Sauce. Reheat zucchinis.
Time for dinner: Dress Salade Nicoise and decorate. Garnish dishes and serve.
Dessert: Delight and entertain your guests by flaming the crepes at the table.

Clockwise from front: Noisettes au Poivre Vert, Courgettes au Beurre, Salade Nicoise

Baking blind

QUICHE LORRAINE

Shortcrust pastry
1½ cups flour, sifted
90 g butter, chopped
1 egg yolk
pinch salt
1 tablespoon cold water
squeeze lemon juice

Filling
250 g rindless bacon, chopped
knob butter
2 eggs
300 mL thickened cream (double cream)
salt, pepper and nutmeg
1 cup grated Gruyere cheese
3 tablespoons chopped chives

Rub butter into flour using fingertips until mixture resembles breadcrumbs. Mix remaining pastry ingredients and add to form a firm dough. Cover with plastic wrap and chill for 30 minutes.

Roll pastry out thinly on lightly floured board, line 6 × 8 cm diameter individual quiche tins. Prick with fork and bake blind by lining with greased greaseproof paper and filling with rice or dried peas. Bake at 200°C (400°F) for 15 minutes. Remove rice and paper and cool.

Fry bacon in butter and drain on absorbent paper. Whip together eggs, cream, seasoning, cheese and chopped chives. Arrange bacon in pastry cases and fill with cream mixture. Cook 15 minutes at 200°C (400°F) and then lower temperature to 180°C (350°F) for further 10 minutes. Serve hot or cold .

NOISETTES AU POIVRE VERT

6 lamb loin fillets
1 tablespoon oil
40 g butter
2 tablespoons brandy
1 cup beef stock
2 tablespoons green peppercorns, drained and rinsed
½ cup cream

Trim fat from lamb fillets. Tie each with string to form a neat log shape. Brush with oil.

Melt butter in frypan until foaming. Add the lamb and brown on all sides turning frequently. Cook 8 minutes then transfer to a heatproof plate, cover with foil and keep warm while preparing sauce.

Deglaze pan with brandy. Add stock and boil until the liquid has reduced to ½ cup. Add remaining ingredients and simmer until thickened slightly.

Remove the string and carve each fillet across the grain into 8 slices. Serve with the Poivre Vert sauce spooned over.

COURGETTES AU BEURRE

750 g zucchini (courgettes), medium-sized
2 tablespoons butter
1 tablespoon chopped parsley
1 teaspoon chopped basil
cracked black pepper
salt

Trim ends off zucchini. Wash and dry. Cut into 2 cm lengths. Drop into boiling salted water for five minutes. Drain and refresh under cold water.

Return to pan with butter, parsley, basil and pepper. Reheat.

Serve hot, sprinkled lightly with salt.

SALADE NICOISE

4 tomatoes, quartered
1 medium onion, sliced thinly
1 green capsicum (pepper), seeded and sliced
1 red capsicum (pepper), seeded and chopped
12 radishes, thinly sliced
4 sticks celery, sliced
1 tablespoon finely chopped basil
1 mignonette lettuce (soft-head lettuce), washed and torn
1 × 185 g can tuna in oil
6 anchovy fillets, chopped
12 stuffed olives, halved
¼ cup vinaigrette dressing

For serving
1 tablespoon capers
2 or 3 hard-boiled eggs, quartered

Prepare vegetables and put into a large salad bowl.

Fork through the tuna in oil, anchovies and olives.

Pour vinaigrette over and toss well.

Decorate salad with capers and eggs. Serve chilled.

CREPES NINETTE

1 cup flour
pinch salt
2 eggs
⅔ cup milk
⅔ cup water
2 tablespoons butter, melted
vanilla essence
2 tablespoons caster sugar
juice of 1 lemon
⅓ cup Grand Marnier

Filling
½ cup butter
½ cup honey
¼ cup sugar
4 sweet apples, peeled cored and sliced

Sift flour and salt into bowl. Blend in eggs and beat in combined milk, water, and melted butter a little at a time, to form a smooth batter. Stir in vanilla essence and rest batter 1 hour.

Grease heated crepe pan with butter and pour enough batter into pan to coat base, making an even circle. Cook over moderate heat until brown. Turn crepe and brown other side, remove from pan and keep warm. Repeat procedure until batter is finished.

The batter may be prepared and crepes made the day before. They may be stored, frozen, between greased paper in stacks of 6.

To make the filling, melt butter, stir in honey and sugar and stir until sugar melts. Add apple slices and cook gently until soft. Strain apple from pan and use to fill crepes.

Return filled crepes to pan and heat gently, basting often with the syrup. Sprinkle with caster sugar and lemon juice. Heat Grand Marnier in a small saucepan, ignite with a taper and pour over crepes in pan. Serve at once. This final step can be done at the last minute and brought to the table in front of the guests.

Stacking pancakes

SIX FOR AN INDIAN REPAST

Spicy Fish Kebabs make a great start to an Indian dinner. The Lamb Curry, an ideal dish to make when entertaining, can be prepared days in advance, frozen and reheated when needed. Cucumber and Yoghurt Salad is served during the meal to refresh the palate.

MENU

Fish Kebabs

Lamb Curry
Mughal Vegetables
Samosas
Cucumber and Yoghurt Salad

Cashew-Nut Fudge

Served with Riesling, Light Ale or Mineral Water

PREPARATION TIMETABLE

Prepare ahead and freeze: Lamb curry, Samosa filling

1 day ahead: Prepare Fish Kebab marinade. Prepare Lamb Curry. Cover and refrigerate overnight. Prepare Samosas. Place apart on floured tray, cover and refrigerate. Prepare Mughal Vegetable ingredients, keeping onion separate. Cover and refrigerate until ready to cook.

6 hours ahead: Cook rice to accompany Lamb Curry. Cool, cover and refrigerate until ready to reheat. Chill white wine.

3 hours ahead: Prepare and marinate fish, cover in refrigerator. Prepare Cucumber and Yoghurt Salad. Cover and refrigerate. Prepare garnishes.

1 hour ahead: Soak wooden kebab skewers in cold water.

30 minutes ahead: Reheat rice in oven. Thread fish onto skewers. Refrigerate until ready to grill. Cook Mughal Vegetables. Keep warm in low oven. Prepare sour cream sauce to accompany vegetables. Cover with plastic wrap to prevent a skin forming.

15 minutes ahead: Reheat Lamb Curry. Deep-fry Samosas. Grill Fish Kebabs, basting continually. Reheat sour cream sauce. Keep hot.

Time for dinner: Arrange food on serving plates. Fluff up rice with a fork. Pour sauce over Mughal Vegetables. Garnish and serve.

Dessert: Cut Cashew-Nut Fudge in diamond shapes. Arrange on a serving plate.

Clockwise from top: Samosas, Lamb Curry, Fish Kebabs, Cucumber and Yoghurt Salad, Mughal Vegetables

FISH KEBABS

1 kg fish fillets, ling or baramundi
2 cloves garlic, crushed
2 onions, very finely chopped
²/₃ cup natural yoghurt
salt to taste
½ teaspoon ginger
½ teaspoon chilli powder
2 teaspoons garam masala
melted butter, for basting

Wash and dry fish and cut into cubes. Combine garlic, onions, yoghurt and spices in bowl. Marinate fish in mixture 2 hours. ☐

Thread fish onto 12 skewers and place under a hot grill, 3–4 minutes each side. Baste fish with melted butter while cooking. Serve hot.

LAMB CURRY

1.25 kg boned shoulder *or* leg lamb
¾ cup flour, seasoned
100 g butter
2 green apples, peeled, cored,
    quartered and sliced
2 onions, chopped
1 tomato, quartered
2 cloves garlic, crushed
1–2 tablespoons curry powder
1¾ cups stock
grated rind and juice of half a lemon
1 teaspoon brown sugar
2 tablespoons desiccated coconut
2 tablespoons sultanas *or* raisins
1 tablespoon flaked almonds
6 cups boiled rice, for serving
red capsicum (peppers) *or* lemon twists,
    to garnish

Trim lamb of excess fat and cut meat into cubes. Toss in flour and shake off any excess.

Melt butter and fry meat until evenly browned. Remove meat and set aside. Add apples to pan with onions, tomato, garlic and curry powder. Fry 2–3 minutes and pour off any excess fat. Add stock. Return meat to pan and add remaining ingredients except almonds. Cover and simmer 2 hours, or until meat is tender. Stir in almonds. ☐

Serve lamb curry with boiled rice. Garnish with red peppers or lemon twists.

MUGHAL VEGETABLES

3 tablespoons oil
2 onions, sliced
¼ teaspoon ground cloves
6 cardamom pods, crushed
5 cm stick cinnamon, broken
2 tablespoons poppy seeds
¼–½ teaspoon chilli powder
2 carrots, sliced
¼ cauliflower, in florets
3 zucchini (courgettes), sliced
150 g green beans, sliced
100 g mushrooms, sliced
¾ cup shredded coconut
¼ cup slivered almonds
¼ cup pistachio nuts
1½ cups beef stock
pinch salt
300 mL sour cream
2 teaspoons lemon juice

Heat oil and cook onion until soft. Add spices, vegetables, nuts and stock. Season with salt and bring to boil. Cover and simmer 15 minutes.

Using slotted spoon, transfer vegetables to serving dish and keep warm.

Add sour cream and lemon juice to liquid in pan, bring to boil and pour over vegetables. Serve hot.

SAMOSAS

4 cups flour
1 teaspoon garam masala
pinch salt
40 g lard
½ cup iced water

Filling
40 g butter
1 onion, chopped finely
1 clove garlic, crushed
1 green chilli, finely chopped
1 red chilli, finely chopped
350 g minced steak
½ teaspoon turmeric
pinch ground ginger
¼ teaspoon chilli powder (optional)
1 teaspoon garam masala
grated rind of 1 lemon
oil for deep frying

To make pastry, sift dry ingredients into a bowl, and rub in lard with fingertips. Add water. Quickly bring mixture together to form a soft dough. Knead on lightly floured board until smooth and elastic. Cover and refrigerate.

Saute onion, garlic and chillies in butter. Add meats and spices and fry until browned. Remove from heat and cool. Divide dough evenly into 24 balls. Roll out each ball to form a circle 12 cm in diameter. Brush edge of circles with water. Place a little filling into one half of each circle and fold edges over to form half moons. Press to seal edges. ☐

Deep-fry samosas in hot oil until golden brown and crisp. Drain and serve immediately.

CUCUMBER AND YOGHURT SALAD

2 cups natural yoghurt
1 cucumber, finely chopped
4 shallots, finely chopped
salt and pepper
1 red chilli, finely chopped
grated rind of half a lemon

Combine yoghurt with cucumber, shallots, salt and pepper and chilli in a bowl. Serve chilled sprinkled with lemon rind.

CASHEW-NUT FUDGE

2 cups sugar
4 tablespoons water
4 tablespoons rose water
250 g raw cashew nuts, ground
250 g butter
2 tablespoons shelled walnuts
½ teaspoon salt
1 tablespoon hot milk

Make a syrup with the sugar and 4 tablespoons water. Add rose water to ground cashews and mix well.

Add cashew mixture to syrup and cook, stirring constantly, till thickened.

Add butter gradually, a little at a time.

Stir in the walnuts, salt and milk and remove from the heat after 1 minute.

Pour into greased square dish and refrigerate. Score into diamond shapes before fudge hardens. Serve cold cut in diamonds.

Lamb Curry and Cucumber and Yoghurt Salad

CHINESE BANQUET FOR EIGHT

Chinese cookery is very much a part of our cuisine today. Once rare and exotic Oriental ingredients and spices are now readily available in specialty shops and supermarkets — which makes shopping for a Chinese banquet relatively easy. By selecting quality ingredients and being well-prepared, you'll find there's plenty of time for enjoying the food and the company.

MENU

Spring Rolls
Sang Choy Bow

Won Ton Soup

Braised Lemon Chicken
Stir-fried Beef and Celery
Fried Rice
Whole Fish with Black Bean Sauce

Almond Float

Served with Rosé

PREPARATION TIMETABLE

Most of the recipes in this banquet need to be cooked just prior to serving. For this reason, an extra hand or two would be very helpful, especially at serving time!

Prepare ahead and freeze: Spring Rolls, won tons.

1 day ahead: Prepare Spring Rolls and won tons. Place on lightly floured trays, cover and refrigerate. Prepare Sang Choy Bow filling. Cover and refrigerate. Prepare chicken pieces for Braised Lemon Chicken. Marinate, covered, in refrigerator. Prepare Almond Float. Refrigerate.

6 hours ahead: Slice beef and celery for Stir-fried Beef and Celery. Store in covered containers in refrigerator. Cook rice. Allow to cool, cover and refrigerate until ready to heat and combine with other ingredients. Prepare whole fish. Cover and refrigerate until ready to steam. Prepare Black Bean Sauce. Cover and refrigerate until required. Cook Braised Lemon Chicken up to stage of stirring in cornflour. Cover and refrigerate. Chill wine.

3 hours ahead: Prepare ingredients for Fried Rice. Wash and dry lettuce leaves for Sang Choy Bow. Keep in refrigerator, wrapped in a damp tea towel. Prepare all garnishes.

1 hour ahead: Marinate shredded beef. Prepare dipping sauce for Spring Rolls. Prepare selection of fresh fruit for Almond Float. Cover and chill in refrigerator.

30 minutes ahead: Heat wok and stir-fry shredded Beef and Celery in batches. Keep warm in oven. Deep-fry Spring Rolls. Keep warm in oven.

15 minutes ahead: Steam fish. Cook won tons and prepare soup. Complete cooking of Fried Rice. Stir in cornflour. Complete cooking of Braised Lemon Chicken.

Time for dinner: Garnish all dishes and serve immediately.

Dessert: Cut Almond Float into diamond shapes.

Clockwise from left: Spring Rolls, Sang Choy Bow, Won Ton Soup, Braised Lemon Chicken, Whole Fish with Black Bean Sauce

SPRING ROLLS

3 tablespoons oil
3 onions, finely chopped
375 g lean ham, diced
375 g bean sprouts
3 teaspoons soy sauce
16 spring roll wrappers
oil for deep-frying
soy sauce, for serving

Alternative filling
375 g minced pork
1½ tablespoons soy sauce
3 tablespoons oil
12 Chinese dried mushrooms, soaked
   and sliced
180 g Chinese cabbage, shredded
375 g water chestnuts, finely chopped

Heat oil in wok and stir-fry onions until transparent. Add ham and bean sprouts and stir-fry gently for 1½ minutes. Stir soy sauce through mixture. Allow to cool.

Spoon 2 tablespoons ham and onion filling onto each spring roll wrapper, fold over at ends and roll up, pressing edges in firmly. Set aside 15 minutes. ☐

Heat oil in wok and deep-fry spring rolls until golden.

Serve hot with soy sauce for dipping.

To cook for alternative filling, season pork with soy sauce and stir-fry in hot oil. Add mushrooms and cabbage and cook for 4 minutes. Stir in water chestnuts, stir and allow to cool.

SANG CHOY BOW

1 tablespoon oil
375 g minced pork
8 lettuce leaves, washed and dried
80 g dried Chinese mushrooms,
   soaked, drained and finely chopped
90 g water chestnuts, finely chopped
9 shallots, finely chopped
400 g canned crabmeat, drained and
   flaked
1½ teaspoons sesame oil
1 tablespoon soy sauce
2 teaspoons oyster sauce
2 tablespoons sherry

Heat oil in wok and stir-fry pork until golden. Stir in mushrooms, water chestnuts, bamboo shoots, shallots and crab. Cook 1 minute.

Combine sesame oil, soy sauce, oyster sauce and sherry and stir into mixture.

Place 2 tablespoons of mixture in the centre of each lettuce leaf. Fold in ends of leaf and roll up to form a neat parcel.
Note: Meat filling and lettuce leaves are generally served separately and guests fill and roll their own lettuce leaves.

WON TON SOUP

16 won ton wrappers
1 dried Chinese mushroom
⅓ cup lean minced pork *or* beef
¼ cup minced prawns
1 water chestnut, minced
3 shallots, minced
½ teaspoon soy sauce
1 teaspoon sherry
pinch of sugar
¼ teaspoon salt
1 egg, lightly beaten
3 cups chicken stock
2 shallots, thinly sliced
1 egg, to garnish

Soak dried mushroom in warm water 20 minutes. Squeeze dry. Remove stalk and mince.

Combine mushroom, pork, prawns, water chestnut, shallots, soy sauce, sherry, sugar and salt and stand 30 minutes.

Place ½ teaspoon of filling on each wrapper (slightly off centre). Brush edges of wrapper with beaten egg, fold in half and press edges together to seal them. Again fold wrapper in half. Pull corners down into crescent shape, overlapping corners. Seal overlap with egg.

Drop won tons into boiling salted water and cook 7 minutes, stirring to prevent sticking. Drain. ☐

Bring chicken stock to the boil. Add won tons and shallots. Top each serving with egg garnish. To make this, beat egg and cook in butter till set. Shred into lengths.

BRAISED LEMON CHICKEN

½ cup soy sauce
3 tablespoons dry sherry
2½ cups lemon juice
6 teaspoons sugar
½ cup oil
6 thin slices fresh ginger
3 cloves garlic, crushed
2 kg assorted chicken pieces, washed
   and dried
3 tablespoons cornflour
1½–2 tablespoons water

Garnish
3 lemons, thinly sliced
1 tablespoon finely chopped parsley
3 small red capsicum (peppers),
   seeded and sliced

Combine soy sauce, sherry, lemon juice and sugar. Pour over chicken pieces and marinate 30 minutes. Drain and reserve marinade.

Heat oil in large pan and add ginger and garlic. Pour over marinade, cover and cook 20–30 minutes stirring occasionally. Just before end of cooking time, blend cornflour and water and stir into sauce to thicken.

Serve hot garnished with lemon slices, parsley and red capsicum.

STIR-FRIED BEEF AND CELERY

1½ kg rump steak, trimmed of excess
   fat
½ cup sherry
½ cup soy sauce
1½ teaspoons sesame oil
¾ cup oil
1 bunch celery, strung and sliced
   diagonally
1½ cups chicken stock
2 tablespoons cornflour
¾ cup water

Cut beef across grain into thin strips. To achieve fine slices, freeze the beef for 10 minutes. This makes it firm and easier to cut.

Combine sherry, soy sauce and sesame oil. Add beef and toss to coat with marinade. Stand 15 minutes, stirring twice.

Heat ½ the oil in a large wok, add beef and stir-fry 3 minutes. (Fry beef in 3 batches). Remove beef and keep warm.

Heat remaining oil in the wok and add celery, stir-frying 1 minute on high. Add chicken stock and simmer 2–3 minutes. Return all beef to wok and heat through.

Blend cornflour with water and marinade and add to wok, stirring until thickened. Serve hot.
Note: 2 woks may have to be used to make such a large quantity at once.

Stir-fried Beef and Celery

FRIED RICE

2 cups long grain rice
2 tablespoons oil
6 shallots, cut into 1 cm pieces
4 eggs, beaten
1 tablespoon water
2 tablespoons soy sauce
2 tablespoons ham, finely diced

Rinse rice in cold water until water runs clear. Put into a saucepan and cover with water 3 cm above the rice. Bring to boil, reduce heat to low and cook, uncovered, until water has evaporated. Place lid on saucepan and cook 7 minutes more over very low heat. Remove from heat and set aside with lid on. Separate grains of rice with fork. □

Heat oil in wok, add shallots and stir-fry 30 seconds. Add rice and stir-fry until heated through. Move rice to sides of wok leaving the base clear.

Combine eggs with water, pour into wok and cook until set. Chop into small pieces and blend into rice. Add soy sauce and stir until well combined. Finally add diced ham, mix well and serve immediately.

WHOLE FISH WITH BLACK BEAN SAUCE

1 kg whole fish (snapper, bream or
    other firm, white-fleshed fish)
salt and pepper
1 slice green ginger
1 tablespoon oil
1 tablespoon canned black beans
1 clove garlic, crushed
1 tablespoon shredded green ginger
½ teaspoon dry sherry
½ teaspoon sugar
2 tablespoons soy sauce
½ cup fish stock or water

Garnish
¼ red capsicum (pepper), seeded and
    cut into strips
shallots
1 tablespoon chopped parsley

Clean and scale fish, trim fins, remove
eyes. Wash and dry with absorbent
paper. Cut two diagonal slashes on
each side of fish to allow even cooking.
Sprinkle salt and pepper into cavity of
fish and rub slice of ginger into slits and
cavity and brush with oil. Grease a serving dish which fits into steamer. Place
steamer over pan of boiling water.
Place fish on serving dish.

Combine beans, garlic and remaining
ginger and add sherry, sugar, soy
sauce and stock. Pour sauce over fish.
Reserve ½ shallots for garnish and
sprinkle remainder over fish. Pour
sauce over. Place dish in steamer,
cover and cook 15–20 minutes, or until
fish flakes easily.

Serve fish hot, garnished with red
capsicum, shallots and parsley.

ALMOND FLOAT

600 mL milk
¼ cup sugar
almond essence to taste
1½ tablespoons gelatine
½ cup water
selection of fresh fruit
1 can lychees

Scald milk and remove from heat. Add
sugar and stir. Cool slightly and add
almond essence.

Sprinkle gelatine over water and
leave until water is absorbed. Dissolve
gelatine over hot water and cool. Stir
into cooled milk mixture. Pour into
lightly oiled lamington tin and refrigerate until set. □

When ready to serve, cut almond-
flavoured gelatine into diamond shapes.
Place fruit in a serving bowl with
diamonds on top.

Whole Fish with Black Bean Sauce

Almond Float

PARTY MENUS

Party food should look special and taste special. It should surprise and delight. But planning an exciting menu is only the first challenge. Having the presentation and service appear effortless is the second.

The bonuses of the following party menus are many — but the most important is ease and preparation of serving. Dishes can be readied completely in advance. The majority can easily be expanded for extra guests. The buffet meals look lavish and expensive, but the costs are quite reasonable.

With the faster pace of life today, the lunch party seems a thing of the past. Yet midday entertaining has a very definite place of its own. On weekends it gives you a chance to see friends who live too far away to attempt a long drive home after dinner, or to entertain family before going off to a concert or sports event. The informality and simplicity of our Spanish-inspired lunch in the garden is entertaining at its least taxing and nerve-wracking. Choose wines that are light and refreshing, a chilled white or rose or a light red, not the big red wine that leads to an afternoon of torpor and somnolence.

Entertaining teenagers

If you want your teenager's party to be a roaring success, all you need to do is provide the kind of food that gets the youth vote of today, then gracefully retire. You can't get more topical than Mexican. Another advantage of a south of the border menu is that you aren't restricted to just a couple of set dishes. We have suggested a choice of two starters, three main courses, a vegetable and two desserts. All the foods have an affinity, which makes a little bit of everything the only way to go. To add flair, you might suggest that everyone turn up as a caballero or muchacha. A teenage sangria is non-alcoholic of course.

The buffet

Buffet food doesn't have to be strictly fork food, but it should be easy to eat (the less bone the better), and served in small manageable proportions. Our buffet menu includes hot and cold and few dishes need last minute attention. White wine and champagne go with every course. If you want to serve something first, make up an easy appetiser that can simply be brought out of the fridge and handed round with such cocktails as dry martinis, Manhattans and champagne and orange.

Clockwise from left: Chilli con Carne, Sangria Punch, Mexican Corn on the Cob, Hot Bean Dip (centre), Fruit Flan, Mexican Chicken, Guacamole

SOUTH-OF-THE BORDER TEENAGE PARTY

Here is an ideal menu for a buffet with flavours that will find favour with all age groups. There's ample food to satisfy hungry teenagers and the Fruit Flan and Sangria Punch are absolute winners for this age group. In fact, just looking at such a delectable and colourful array of food is enough to stimulate young appetites.

MENU

Guacamole
Hot Bean Dip

Mexican Chicken
Chilli con Carne
Spicy Mexican Rice and Sausages
Mexican Corn on the Cob

Fruit Flan

Served with non-alcoholic Sangria

PREPARATION TIMETABLE

Make ahead and freeze: Mexican Chicken, Chilli con Carne.
1 day ahead: Prepare Guacamole and store in screwtop jar (including avocado seed) in refrigerator. Prepare and cook Mexican Chicken and Chilli con Carne. Cover and refrigerate until ready to reheat and serve. Prepare and bake pastry bases. When cool, cover flan tins and refrigerate until ready to fill. Prepare and briefly cook vegetable sticks to serve with Guacamole and refrigerate in a plastic bag. Fill ice cube trays and freeze for Sangria Punch.
6 hours ahead: Prepare Spicy Mexican Rice and Sausages up to stage of adding tomatoes. Cover and refrigerate until ready to reheat and serve. Prepare topping mixture and corn cobs for Mexican Corn on the Cob. Chill beverages.
3 hours ahead: Prepare filling and fruit topping for Fruit Flan. Puree peaches,

slice apples and squeeze juices for Sangria Punch.
1 hour ahead: Fill and decorate Fruit Flans. Prepare garnishes. Slice avocado (pour over lemon juice to prevent browning) and grate cheese for Hot Bean Dip.
30 mintes ahead: Spoon Guacamole into serving bowl and arrange vegetable sticks on a platter. Assemble and bake Hot Bean Dip. Cook Corn Cobs and keep warm in oven. Reheat Mexican Chicken, Chilli con Carne, Spicy Mexican Rice and Sausages.
15 minutes ahead: Make glaze for Fruit Flans and brush over fruit. Refrigerate until serving time. Combine Sangria Punch ingredients in a punch bowl.
Time for dinner: Spoon topping over corn cobs, garnish and serve immediately. Garnish other dishes and serve.
Dessert: Transfer flans to serving plates, slice and serve.

Mexican Chicken

GUACAMOLE

4 ripe avocados
juice of 2 lemons *or* limes
1 teaspoon salt (optional)
2 large onions, grated
2 cloves garlic, crushed
2 teaspoons curry powder
pinch cayenne
few drops Tabasco sauce (optional)
chopped red chillies for garnish
taco or corn chips for serving

Mash avocados with fork or blend in food processor. Add lemon or lime juice and salt. Add remaining ingredients to avocado. Cover with plastic wrap and chill to serve. Spoon into two bowls before serving. ☐
Note: If guacamole is to be used for salad dressing, omit curry and blend in a little olive oil to dilute the mixture, or mayonnaise instead of oil may also be used. Garnish with chopped red chillies. Serve with taco chips and vegetable sticks.

For this versatile Mexican dish it is good to look for over-ripe avocados. These can often be purchased cheaply, and the mixture can be made and frozen for later use. Guacamole can be served as a starter on a lettuce leaf, or as a party dip to be eaten with taco chips. If preparing in advance mash avocados with a wooden spoon and store the finished guacamole in a jar with the avocado seeds. This will prevent discolouring.

HOT BEAN DIP

2 packets corn chips
250 g Cheddar cheese, grated
300 mL sour cream
1 × 425 g can refried beans
1 avocado, sliced

Place a layer of corn chips on a heatproof serving platter. Sprinkle with some Cheddar cheese and top with alternating layers of sour cream, refried beans and more corn chips. Sprinkle remaining cheese on the top.

Bake at 150°C (300°F) for 30 minutes or until heated through and cheese has melted.

Serve garnished with avocado.

MEXICAN CHICKEN

14 chicken pieces
seasoned flour
¼ cup oil
3 large onions, sliced
2 cloves garlic, crushed
½–1 teaspoon chilli powder, to taste
1 tablespoon sesame seeds
½ teaspoon oregano
¾ cup dry red wine
1 cup chicken stock
1 cup slivered almonds
1 cup stuffed olives, sliced
1 × 450 g can corn kernels, drained
1 red capsicum (pepper), diced
1 teaspoon cornflour

Dust chicken pieces lightly with flour. Heat oil and brown chicken in pan on both sides. Place in casserole.

Add onions and garlic to pan. Cook till soft. Stirring to prevent sticking. Stir in chilli powder, sesame seeds, oregano, wine and stock. Then pour this over chicken pieces.

Cover casserole and cook in preheated oven at 180°C (350°F) for 1 hour. Add remaining ingredients except cornflour. Blend cornflour with a little liquid from the casserole dish, pour over chicken.

Return chicken to oven for 10–15 minutes or until sauce thickened. Serve hot.

CHILLI CON CARNE

¼ cup oil
3 onions, chopped
2 cloves garlic, crushed
1 kg minced beef
780 g canned red kidney beans, drained
1 × 800 g can peeled tomatoes
2 teaspoons paprika
2 teaspoons chilli powder, or to taste

Heat oil in large pan, add onions and garlic and gently saute until soft. Add minced beef and fry until evenly browned. Stir in beans, tomatoes paprika and chilli powder. Cover and simmer gently for 45–50 minutes. Adjust seasoning and serve hot.

SPICY MEXICAN RICE AND SAUSAGES

500 g pork sausages
150 g butter
500 g frankfurts
2 large onions, chopped
1 red capsicum (pepper), seeded and finely chopped
1 green capsicum (pepper), seeded and finely chopped
1½ cups long grain rice
chilli powder, to taste
1 litre chicken stock
2 tablespoons tomato paste
1 cup canned corn kernels, drained
freshly ground black pepper
4 tomatoes, cut into wedges
2 teaspoons snipped chives, for garnish

Boil pork sausages in water for 10 minutes (to remove excess fat) and drain.

Melt butter and fry frankfurts and sausages over medium heat 4–5 minutes, shaking pan to prevent sticking. Remove sausages from pan and cut into chunky pieces.

Fry onions and capsicum until onions are lightly golden. Add rice and chilli powder and cook over gentle heat 2–3 minutes, stirring all the time.

Add stock, tomato paste, corn, sausage pieces and seasoning. Bring to boil, stir well, reduce heat and simmer gently 15 minutes until rice is tender and liquid absorbed.

Add tomatoes to pan for the last 5 minutes of cooking. ☐

Sprinkle with snipped chives and serve.

MEXICAN CORN ON THE COB

4 hard-boiled eggs
40 g butter, softened
4 tablespoons thickened cream (double cream)
½ teaspoon Tabasco
2 tablespoons chopped parsley
salt and pepper
5 corn cobs
4 teaspoons sugar

Mash eggs with fork till smooth. Blend in butter then stir in cream, Tabasco, parsley and seasoning to taste.

Cut each corn cob into three pieces. Cook in boiling water with sugar 20–30 minutes or until tender. Drain.

Serve cobs hot, topped with egg and butter mixture.

FRUIT FLAN

Pastry bases
4 sheets ready rolled shortcrust pastry
1 egg, beaten

Filling
500 g cream cheese, softened
1 teaspoon cinnamon
1 cup caster sugar
juice and grated rind of a lemon

Topping
1 honeydew melon, seeded and
  scooped into balls
300 g muscat grapes, stems removed
½ rock melon (cantaloupe), seeded and
  scooped into balls
½ honeydew melon, seeded and
  scooped into balls
2 punnets strawberries, hulled
2 kiwifruit, peeled and sliced

Fruit Flan

Glaze
1 cup apricot jam, warmed and sieved
½ cup orange juice or water

Preheat oven to 200°C (400°F). Join 2 pastry sheets together, pressing join firmly. Repeat with remaining 2 sheets. Grease 2 × 22 cm flan tins, press pastry gently into base and bake blind 10 minutes. Remove baking beans and prick pastry base with fork. Cool completely before filling. Do not fill more than 3 hours before serving.

Combine filling ingredients and beat until smooth and creamy. Spoon equal amounts into the flan cases and smooth top of each with a spatula. Refrigerate until firm — about 1 hour.

Top with decoratively arranged fruit.

Combine glaze ingredients and lightly brush over fruit. Chill before serving.

SANGRIA PUNCH

1.6 kg canned peaches, pureed and
  chilled
2 apples, cored and thinly sliced
1 teaspoon mixed spice
2 bottles non-alcoholic red wine, chilled
sugar (optional)
juice of 4 oranges
½ cup lemon juice
ice cubes

Place the peach puree and apples in a punchbowl and pour in the wine. Add the mixed spice and a few teaspoons of sugar if a sweeter drink is preferred. Add the lemon and orange juices and plenty of ice cubes and stir gently with a wooden spoon until the wine is thoroughly chilled.

BUFFET FOR TEN TO TWELVE

Buffets are the ideal solution when entertaining larger groups. The following recipes help make the table a feast for the eyes, and the appetite. Most of the recipes can be made the day before.

MENU

Ham Mousse with Cumberland Sauce
Seafood Fettuccine
Turkey Breast with Sour Cherry Sauce
Broccoli with Horseradish
Cassata Torte
Cold Citrus Chiffon

Served with Chardonnay and Cabernet Sauvignon

PREPARATION TIMETABLE

1 day ahead: Prepare Ham Mousse and refrigerate until ready to unmould and serve. Prepare Cumberland Sauce, cover and refrigerate. Prepare turkey breasts. If serving cold, bake, cool, cover and refrigerate. Prepare Sour Cherry Sauce. Cover and refrigerate. Prepare Cassata Torte cakes and buttercreams. Store cakes in an airtight container. Cover and refrigerate buttercreams. Prepare Cold Citrus Souffle.

6 hours ahead: Prepare and bake Seafood with Fettuccine. Cover and refrigerate. Blanch broccoli and prepare horseradish sauce. Cover and refrigerate. Chill beverages.

3 hours ahead: Assemble and decorate Cassata Torte. Chill in refrigerator. Prepare garnishes.

1 hour ahead: Remove Seafood with Fettuccine from refrigerator to return to room temperature. Whip extra cream for souffle, refrigerate. If serving Turkey Breasts hot, bake in oven and keep warm until ready to carve. If serving cold, carve, arrange on serving platter, cover and refrigerate until serving time.

30 minutes ahead: Reheat Seafood with Fettuccine. Unmould Ham Mousse onto a serving plate. Decorate and chill until serving time. Open red wine.

15 minutes ahead: Carve hot turkey breasts and keep warm in a low oven. Reheat broccoli. Arrange in a serving dish mask with sauce.

Time for dinner: Arrange hot turkey breasts on a serving platter. Dress hot or cold turkey breasts with sauce. Garnish and serve.

Desserts: Remove paper collar from souffle dish. Pipe cream on top and decorate. Transfer the Cassata Torte to a serving platter. Slice this impressive dessert at the table.

Clockwise from far left: Cassata Torte, Cumberland Sauce, Ham Mousse, Turkey Breast with Sour Cherry Sauce, Broccoli with Horseradish Seafood Fettuccine

HAM MOUSSE

¾ cup finely ground ham
1 cup beef consomme
1 cup tomato juice
½ teaspoon paprika
1½ tablespoons gelatine softened in 4
    tablespoons cold beef stock
2 cups cream, beaten to hold shape
1 tablespoon sherry
salt

Precoat a 6-cup mould with clear aspic. Allow to set. Process the ham and mix with consomme, tomato juice and paprika. Bring to the boil in saucepan. Add gelatine mixture and stir until dissolved. Strain mixture through fine sieve. Cool, stirring, over ice. When thickened slightly, add beaten cream flavoured with sherry and salt to taste.

Fill the mould with mousse and chill thoroughly until set. Unmould onto a serving plate. Decorate with watercress and cherry tomatoes. The cherry tomatoes may be hollowed out and filled with piped cream cheese with tiny shreds of preserved ginger mixed through.

Serve with Cumberland Sauce (see recipe).

CUMBERLAND SAUCE

1 cup redcurrant jelly
1 shallot
1 tablespoon slivered lemon and orange
    rind mixed.
¼ cup port
1 tablespoon lemon juice
1 tablespoon orange juice
¼ teaspoon dry mustard
salt and cayenne

Melt the redcurrant jelly, add the remaining ingredients and simmer gently for 3–4 minutes. Allow to cool and thicken. □

SEAFOOD FETTUCCINE

500 g thin egg noodles
120 g butter
700 g filleted white fish ,cut into 2 cm
    pieces
white part of a small leek, sliced
⅔ cup dry white wine
1 cup fish stock
1 cup Bechamel Sauce (see recipe)
1 cup cream
½ teaspoon salt
pinch of cayenne
1 teaspoon lemon juice
250 g prawns and scallops
180 g parmesan cheese, grated
125 g butter, melted

Cook noodles in boiling water 8 minutes. Drain, rinse and cool slightly. Toss 40 g butter through and cover.

Heat remaining butter in pan, add fish and saute with sliced leek. Add wine and fish stock, bring to boil and simmer 1 minute. Remove fish and reduce liquid by ½. Add Bechamel Sauce, cream, salt, cayenne and cook gently until sauce is smooth and glossy but not thick. Remove from heat, add lemon juice and strain.

Saute prawns and scallops gently in butter. Do not overcook. Combine fish, prawns and scallops.

Place ⅓ of noodles in an oblong casserole, cover with ½ the fish mixture and ⅓ of the grated cheese, sauce and melted butter. Repeat for second layer. Top with the remaining noodles, sauce and melted butter.

Bake in a hot oven 200°C (400°F) 10–15 minutes until golden.
Note: This dish may be prepared earlier in the day, covered with aluminium foil and kept in refrigerator. Allow to return to room temperature before reheating.

BECHAMEL SAUCE

1 tablespoon butter
1 tablespoon flour
1 cup milk

Melt butter in a medium-sized pan. When foaming, add flour and stir over low heat 3 minutes. Remove from heat and gradually add milk, stirring constantly. Return to heat and cook, stirring until boiling. Cook a further 3 minutes.

Seafood Fettuccine

TURKEY BREAST

4 whole turkey fillets
½ cup brandy
2 tablespoons dry mustard
1 tablespoon melted butter
watercress for garnish (optional)

Forcemeat
4 cups breadcrumbs *or* cooked rice
60 g chopped prunes
60 g chopped dried apricots
2 small onions, chopped and sauteed
salt and pepper
finely grated orange rind and lemon rind
mixed herbs
1 egg, beaten
1 tablespoon sour cherry juice, reserved
    from sauce recipe

Mix all the forcemeat ingredients together, binding with the egg and 1 tablespoon sour cherry juice.

Open out the turkey fillets and flatten slightly. Brush the inside of the breast with ½ the brandy and sprinkle over the mustard. Stuff with the forcemeat and skewer in place. Brush with remaining brandy and mustard. Place in baking pan, cover with greased aluminium foil and bake at 160°C (325°F) 20–30 minutes basting during cooking time.

Remove the breasts from oven. Allow to stand 10 minutes before carving. Slice and arrange on serving platter. Dress with a little Sour Cherry Sauce and serve rest separately. Garnish with watercress if desired.

Note: The dish may be prepared beforehand if it is served cold.

Large turkey breasts may be used for this recipe to give your buffet a more lavish approach. These need to be ordered at least 1 day in advance from a fresh chicken shop or frozen food outlet. Chicken breasts make a suitable substitute. Use 8 breasts, make a pocket in 1 side of each breast and stuff. Secure with toothpicks and bake according to the recipe. Carve each breast on the diagonal for serving.

Turkey Breast with Sour Cherry Sauce, Broccoli with Horseradish

SOUR CHERRY SAUCE

1 × 450 g can pitted sour cherries
2 tablespoons brandy
2 tablespoons brown sugar
2 tablespoons malt vinegar
1 cup strong chicken stock
½ cup orange juice
2 tablespoons grated orange rind
grated rind and juice of half a lemon
2 tablespoons cornflour

Drain cherries and set aside reserving 1 tablespoon juice for turkey forcemeat. Mix remaining cherry juice with brandy.

Boil brown sugar and malt vinegar until caramelised. When cool, add chicken stock, orange juice and rind, lemon juice and brandy and cherry juice.

Dissolve 2 tablespoons cornflour with water add to sauce and cook to thicken. Stir in pan juices from turkey, first removing fat and straining. Add cherries and serve.

BROCCOLI WITH HORSERADISH

80 g butter, melted
¾ cup mayonnaise
2 tablespoons horseradish cream
2 tablespoons grated onion
¼ teaspoon salt
¼ teaspoon dry mustard
paprika
1 large bunch fresh broccoli *or* 2
    packets frozen
1 tablespoon lemon juice
20 g butter

Combine melted butter, mayonnaise, horseradish, grated onion, salt, mustard and paprika and chill.

Boil broccoli 8 minutes, or until crispy tender. Drain and refresh in cold water. Reheat with a little lemon and butter and serve with sauce.

To collar-line a souffle dish, place a double thickness of greaseproof paper around the outside of dish to make sides higher. Secure with string.

CASSATA TORTE

8 eggs
1 cup caster sugar
160 g unsalted butter
1½ cup flour, sifted
1 teaspoon baking powder

Buttercream
2 tablespoons instant coffee powder
½ cup warm milk
300 g butter
5 cups icing sugar, sieved
200 g glace cherries
1 × 325 g can pineapple pieces, drained
60 g angelica, chopped
3 tablespoons kirsch
⅔ cup chopped nuts
½ cup cream, whipped

Preheat oven to 190°C (375°F). Place eggs and sugar in a heatproof bowl over hot water. Whisk until thick and whisk leaves trail when removed from mixture.

Cassata Torte

Remove from heat and continue to whisk until cool.

Melt unsalted butter and cool but do not allow to set. Gently fold small quantities of flour into egg mixture alternately with melted butter. Finish with flour and baking powder. Pour mixture into 2 × 20cm greased and paper-lined cake tins, bake for 35–40 minutes. Cool on wire rack.

To make buttercream, dissolve coffee powder in a little of the warm milk. Cream butter and beat in sugar a little at a time. Beat in coffee flavouring. Add sufficient warm milk to soften mixture. Reserve 9 cherries and 9 pineapple pieces. Stir chopped angelica, remaining cherries and pineapple into half of the buttercream.

Split each cake into 3 layers. Sprinkle with kirsch and sandwich together with fruity buttercream. Coat top and sides with plain buttercream, reserving some for piping.

Decorate cake with reserved buttercream and fruit. If the weather is hot keep refrigerated until serving. □

Cold Citrus Chiffon

COLD CITRUS CHIFFON

6 eggs, separated
¾ cup sugar
1½ cups orange juice
2 tablespoons lemon juice
2½ tablespoons powdered gelatine softened in ½ cup orange juice and dissolved over hot water
1 teaspoon grated lemon zest
2 tablespoons orange zest
½ tablespoon orange liqueur
600 mL thickened cream (double cream)
¼ cup sugar
extra 300 mL cream for decoration or to serve separately (optional)
8 orange segments
shredded rind of one orange

Lightly oil a 1.7 litre souffle dish. Prepare a greaseproof collar to fit around and extend 8 cm above the rim. Lightly oil, tie and tape securely in position.

Beat egg yolks and sugar in a bowl 10 minutes or until mousse-like. Add orange and lemon juices gradually. Stir in the dissolved gelatine. Add lemon and orange zests and liqueur. Cool in refrigerator until mixture is a soft gel-like consistency. Do not allow it to set. Remove bowl and let rise to room temperature.

Whip the thickened cream until soft peaks form.

Whip the egg whites until soft peaks form and beat in the ¼ cup sugar gradually until of meringue consistency. Fold egg whites and cream into the orange mixture alternately. Pour into souffle dish and refrigerate 3 hours until set. □

Before serving, remove paper collar from around souffle dish. Whip extra cream and pipe on top of souffle. Decorate with orange segments and shredded orange rind.

LUNCH IN THE GARDEN FOR EIGHT

Eating out-of-doors always makes you appreciate good food even more. Finding a shady part of the garden, decorating an elegant table and serving colourful food will be more inviting to your guests than a no-fuss lunch inside. The no fuss menu will care for itself so relax in the fresh air without worrying about stove top failures.

MENU

Gazpacho

Cannelloni with Olives
Tomato and Feta Cheese Salad

Paella
Baked Bream and Orange

Creme Caramel

Served with Rosé

PREPARATION TIMETABLE

1 day ahead: Prepare Gazpacho. Store in a covered container in refrigerator. Prepare garlic flavoured croutons and keep in an airtight container. Fill ice cube trays and freeze. Prepare Cannelloni with Olives. Cover and refrigerate until ready to heat and serve. Prepare Creme Caramel and cook. When cooled, chill in refrigerator.

6 hours before: Prepare vegetables for garnishing and serving with Gazpacho. Chill in refrigerator. Prepare stuffing mixture for Baked Bream Orange. Refrigerate until ready to use. Prepare fish. Cover and refrigerate. Chill beverages.

3 hours ahead: Prepare Tomato and Fetta Cheese Salad. Prepare salad dressing. Prepare seafood, chicken and other ingredients for Paella.

1 hour ahead: Prepare garnishes. Whip cream for Creme Caramel.

30 minutes ahead: Cook Paella and Cannelloni with Olives. Complete preparation of Baked Bream Orange.

15 minutes ahead: Bake fish. Place prepared vegetables to accompany Gazpacho into serving bowls.

Time for dinner: Pour soup over ice cubes and top with croutons. Garnish and serve Paella, Cannelloni with Olives and Baked Bream Orange. Pour dressing over salad and serve.

Dessert: Turn out Creme Caramel moulds onto serving plates, garnish and serve.

Clockwise from left: Cannelloni with Olives, Gazpacho, Baked Bream and Orange, Tomato and Feta Cheese Salad, Paella

GAZPACHO

2–3 cloves garlic, crushed
1 teaspoon salt
1 tablespoon sugar
2 teaspoons cumin
1 tablespoon paprika
120 mL olive oil
2 tablespoons wine vinegar
pinch cayenne pepper
1.6 kg canned peeled tomatoes
1 litre chicken stock (can be made with stock cubes)
1 cucumber, peeled and diced
1 bunch shallots, chopped
1 green capsicum (pepper), diced
2 cups croutons

Combine and blend first 8 ingredients. When thick, add tomatoes and blend. Pour into large bowl and add stock. Add cucumber dice, cover and place in refrigerator for several hours to chill. □

To serve, place ice cubes in a bowl, pour over soup and sprinkle shallots and capsicum on top. Serve with croutons.

Baked Bream and Orange, Paella

CANNELLONI WITH OLIVES

8 cannelloni tubes, ready to bake
1 tablespoon oil
2 onions, chopped
350 g minced beef
1½ tablespoons tomato paste
1 teaspoon chopped fresh basil
1 teaspoon sugar
8 stuffed olives
freshly ground black pepper
1 tomato, thinly sliced

Sauce
30 g butter
¼ cup flour
1½ cups milk
¼ cup cream
1 teaspoon prepared mustard
salt and pepper to taste
1 cup grated cheddar cheese

Preheat oven to 190°C (375°F). Heat oil and saute onion until soft. Add minced beef and cook until browned. Stir in tomato paste, basil and sugar. Chop 6 olives and add to beef mixture; season with salt and pepper.

Using piping bag or spoon, fill cannelloni tubes with mixture. Place in shallow ovenproof dish.

Melt butter in a saucepan, add flour and cook 1 minute. Remove from heat and add liquid gradually. Return to heat and simmer 2–3 minutes stirring constantly until thickened. Flavour with mustard, salt and pepper. Stir in most of cheese, reserving a little for the top.

Pour sauce over cannelloni, sprinkle with remaining cheese and bake 20 minutes. Decorate with sliced olives and tomato. Serve hot, 1 cannelloni per person.

TOMATO AND FETA CHEESE SALAD

1 cos lettuce, well-washed
2 tomatoes, cut into quarters
250 g feta cheese, cubed
1 white onion, sliced
½ cup black olives
¼ cup Walnut Dressing (see recipe)

Line a salad bowl with the lettuce and top with remaining ingredients. Cover and chill well before serving.

PAELLA

3 tablespoons oil
2 onions, sliced
1 clove garlic, crushed
1 cup long grain rice
4 cups tomato juice, boiling
¼ teaspoon turmeric
pinch of freshly ground black pepper
2 cups cooked, cubed chicken
250 g prawns, shelled and deveined
6 mussels, in the shell, scrubbed and
    bearded
1 cup frozen peas
½ cup stuffed olives, sliced

Heat oil and saute onion and garlic
lightly. Add rice, tomato juice, turmeric
and pepper. Cook, stirring occasionally,
covered for 20 minutes until rice is tender and liquid is absorbed.

Stir in chicken, prawns, mussels and
peas and cook. Heat until prawns turn
pink, stirring occasionally.

Stir through olives. Serve hot from
pan.

Creme Caramel

BAKED BREAM AND ORANGE

2 large oranges, peeled and segmented
40 g butter
1 large onion, finely sliced
2 cloves garlic, crushed
2 tablespoons parsley, chopped
freshly ground black pepper
1 cup bean sprouts
½ cup slivered almonds, toasted
½ cup red and green capsicum
    (pepper), seeded and chopped
2 whole silver bream (about 1 kg each)
1¼ cups orange juice
Italian parsley, to garnish

Dice ½ the orange segments. Lightly
saute onion and garlic with butter. Add
diced orange segments, parsley and
seasonings and cook lightly a further 2
minutes. Add bean sprouts, almonds
and capsicum.

Trim fish tail and fins using kitchen
scissors and remove any scales still at-
tached. Season cavity then stuff each
with above orange and onion mixture.
Place fish in large ovenproof dish and
cover with orange juice. Top with buttered greaseproof paper. Bake at 180°C
(350°F) for approximately 20 minutes or
until flesh flakes easily. Arrange remaining orange segments over fish and
garnish with parsley.

Serve hot dividing each fish into 4
equal pieces.

CREME CARAMEL

2¾ cups sugar
½ cup water
1 egg
1 egg yolk
3 tablespoons water
vanilla
700 mL milk
Spun sugar (*see recipe*)
300 mL cream, whipped for serving

Bring ½ cup water and 1 cup sugar to
the boil in a heavy-based saucepan.
Boil without stirring until mixture is a
rich golden caramel colour. Pour caramel into 1 large mould, coating the base
and sides, or into 8 individual ramekin
dishes. Set aside to cool.

Preheat oven to 180°C (350°F). Combine eggs, 1¾ cups sugar, 3 tablespoons water and vanilla essence. Heat
milk, without boiling, and gradually
whisk into egg mixture. Strain and pour
into mould. Place mould in a baking tin
half-filled with water and bake 40–50
minutes, or until set. Individual moulds
will only take 20 minutes to cook. Test
by inserting a butter knife into the custard. If the knife comes out clean, the
custard is set. ☐

Chill thoroughly before turning out
onto serving dish. Pour any caramel remaining in the mould around the dish
and decorate with spun sugar if desired.
Serve with whipped cream.

SPUN SUGAR

1 cup caster sugar
pinch of cream of tartar
½ cup water

Combine all the ingredients in a small
saucepan and heat, gently stirring until
the sugar dissolves. Using a wet pastry
brush, brush away any remaining crystals from the side of the pan as these
will cause the syrup to crystallise.

Increase the heat and boil until a rich
golden colour. Allow to cool slightly.
Working over sheets of baking paper
dip two forks into the syrup, join
together then draw apart to form fine
threads of toffee. Work quickly before
the toffee sets and remember that it is
very hot. When all the toffee has been
used carefully lift the threads from the
paper and place a little on top of each
cream caramel.

Note: Do not attempt this if the weather
is humid as the spun sugar will dissolve
within moments of making. Prepare just
before serving.

ENTERTAINING WITH EASE

Dining on a more casual level puts everyone at ease. Conversation flows smoothly, and guests are relaxed enough to treat your house as their own. But a little strategy is necessary to make an informal meal a success: keep serving pieces to a minimum to avoid clutter; plan only a few courses; and choose recipes that will allow as much do-ahead preparation as possible. Our six menus follow these guidelines, and all have enough show-off potential to make your next laid-back entertaining affair an event.

The pantry shelf
The pantry shelf, thoughtfully stocked and maintained, is a great aid to informal and impromptu entertaining. Party staples include: pasta, canned crab, tuna and salmon, green peppercorns, UHT or canned cream, ham, tomato puree, olives, party nuts, canned cherries and mangoes, dried fruit and pulses, rice, frozen puff and filo pastry. Nothing is more gratifying to find how quickly a meal can materialise from the pantry shelf to go with spur-of-the moment invitation.

Create a cooking party
If all your friends appreciate good food and like to cook, turn an informal occasion into a cooking party. Make sure you have enough utensils for everyone, or let them bring their own. Each guest should have a recipe and be familiar with the location of pots, pans, moulds and other necessary implements. Assign each part of the meal to a specific participant at a certain time with a precise place to work. The camaraderie that a cooking "bee" engenders makes great food with great friends an even more memorable get-together.

The freezer: ideal for unflappable entertaining
The freezer is also a help in beating those last minute dinner blues. Develop a plan and use slow days to make stock, toast croutons or make a stack of crepes. Freeze in meal-size quantities and keep an inventory. When you are preparing dishes specifically for entertaining, undercook slightly. Reheating will bring them to their optimum state. Good freezer entertaining assets include: pureed avocado, bearnaise sauce, pounded chicken breasts, game birds or trout, lasagne and cannelloni, meat balls, pie crusts, pasta and marinana sauces and vegetable purees.

Casseroles: a boon for the busy cook
Casseroles are just too good to be true for informal entertaining. They can be made ahead, reheated, even mistreated and still come out tasting great. But because stews and casseroles are so reliable, some cooks feel they aren't quite the thing to serve to guests. But a party stew can provide you with a world of flavours to choose from — red cooked beef from China, a spicy Malaysian curry, Hungarian goulash and wine-braised sauerkraut or mustard-laced French rabbit casserole. Whatever its origin, fork tender meat in a harmonious sauce is a boon for a busy, informal cook.

Sherried Mushroom Soup, Fettuccine with Anchovy and Tuna Sauce

DINNER FOR FOUR FROM THE PANTRY SHELF

Keeping your pantry well stocked with staple ingredients lets you create a quick dinner party with the turn of an opener. The added bonus of being prepared to face the unexpected minimises shopping time. With canned soups, seafood, pulses, purees, vegetables and fruit as basic pantry supplies, you can face any emergency with equanimity.

MENU

Sherried Mushroom Soup

Fettuccine with Anchovy and Tuna Sauce
Canned Vegetable Souffle
Insalata Colori

Apricot Delight
Turkish Biscuits

Served with Chardonnay

PREPARATION TIMETABLE

1 day ahead: Prepare Apricot Delight, cover and keep in refrigerator. Toast almonds. Make Turkish Biscuits and store in airtight container.
6 hours ahead: Place any white wines in the refrigerator to chill.
3 hours ahead: Make the soup. Cover soup bowl with plastic wrap — wrap should sit on top of soup to prevent skin forming — and chill until ready to heat and serve. Make croutons and chop chives.
1 hour ahead: Make the Anchovy and Tuna Sauce and set aside. Prepare the Vegetable Souffle up to the point of adding the eggs and cream. Spoon the Apricot Delight into individual serving dishes and chill.
30 minutes ahead: Complete the Vegetable Souffle and cook.
15 minutes ahead: Reheat Sherried Mushroom Soup. Warm soup bowls. Cook fettuccine. Drain and keep warm until ready to serve.
Time for dinner: Garnish soup and serve.

Clockwise from left: Insalata Colori, Fettuccine with Anchovy and Tuna Sauce, Sherried Mushroom Soup, Canned Vegetable Souffle

SHERRIED MUSHROOM SOUP

30 g butter
250 g mushrooms, finely chopped
salt and pepper
1 × 440 g can mushroom soup
    concentrate
1½ cups milk
2 tablespoons cream
2 tablespoons sherry
4 teaspoons sour cream
croutons and chopped chives for
    serving

Melt butter in pan and cook mushrooms 4 minutes until tender. Add salt and pepper to taste. Pour in soup, stirring lightly. Gradually add milk and keep stirring until soup has coloured and developed flavour. Add cream and sherry.☐

Serve in warmed soup bowls. Garnish with 1 teaspoon sour cream, croutons and a sprinkling of chopped chives.

FETTUCCINE WITH ANCHOVY AND TUNA SAUCE

500 g fresh fettuccine
3 tablespoons olive oil

Sauce
1 × 425 g can peeled tomatoes,
    drained and chopped
1 × 50 g can anchovy fillets
1 × 185 g can tuna in oil, flaked
½ cup black olives, chopped
3 cloves garlic, crushed
2 tablespoons fresh lemon juice
freshly ground black pepper
2 tablespoons Italian parsley, chopped
grated Parmesan cheese, for garnish

Cook fettuccine in boiling water for approximately 3–5 minutes until al dente. Drain. Mix with 1 tablespoon oil. Keep hot.

Combine the tomatoes, anchovies, tuna, olives, garlic, lemon juice and pepper. Stir in rest of oil gradually.

Toss fettuccine and parsley with sauce until well coated. Serve Parmesan cheese separately if desired.

CANNED VEGETABLE SOUFFLE

130 g canned corn kernels, drained
340 g canned asparagus spears,
    drained
1 tablespoon chopped parsley
1 tablespoon chopped chives
1½ cups grated Romano cheese
strips of red pimiento
4 eggs
1 cup cream
salt and pepper
pinch chilli powder
4 lean bacon rashers, remove rind and
    dice bacon

Grease a large round ovenproof dish and arrange a layer of corn and asparagus. Sprinkle over ½ the parsley and chives and top with 1 cup of cheese. Add pimiento strips. Arrange second layer of corn and asparagus.

Beat together eggs, cream and seasonings, pour over the vegetables and top with rest of cheese. Sprinkle bacon and remaining parsley over the mixture and bake 30–35 minutes at 220°C (425°F) until souffle has risen and is golden brown. Serve immediately.

INSALATA COLORI

1 lettuce
3 sticks celery
½ bunch radish

Dressing
¼ teaspoon salt
1 teaspoon French mustard
1 tablespoon vinegar
1 teaspoon caster sugar
3 tablespoons oil
black pepper

Wash and dry lettuce and tear into small pieces. Slice celery and radishes. Mix, cover and chill until required.

Combine dressing ingredients and add to salad and toss just before serving.

APRICOT DELIGHT

1 cup dried apricots
1½ cups water
½ cup sugar
½ teaspoon grated lemon rind
½ teaspoon grated orange rind

Garnish
2 cups cream, whipped
¼ cup slivered or flaked almonds,
    lightly toasted

Place apricots in water with sugar, bring to boil and cook gently for 25 minutes. Add grated citrus rind. Allow to cool.

Puree apricots in blender. Place pureed apricots in a bowl and gently fold in whipped cream. Chill. Spoon apricot mixture into serving glasses. Decorate with cream and toasted almonds.

Serve with Turkish Biscuits (*see recipe*).

TURKISH BISCUITS

2 egg whites
½ cup caster sugar
2 cups desiccated coconut
1 teaspoon baking powder
3 tablespoons white breadcrumbs
1 teaspoon lemon essence
2 tablespoons pistachio nuts, finely
    chopped

Whisk egg whites until stiff. Add sugar and continue to whisk until glossy and sugar is dissolved. Stir in remaining ingredients and mix well.

Drop mixture onto greased baking trays in large teaspoonsful 3 cm apart. Bake at 140°C (250°F) for 20–30 minutes until a light golden colour. Remove and cool on racks.☐
Note: The biscuits will keep in an airtight container.

Apricot Delight

DINNER IN AN HOUR FOR TWO

Racing home from the office laden with shopping and raw ingredients, expecting to turn out a gourmet meal in minutes is a sure way to turn a dinner for two into disaster. The following menu is designed to simplify entertaining for working people by using tender spatchcocks, salad, and a very quick peachy mousse.

MENU

Potted Crab with Toast Triangles

Grilled Spatchcocks with Red Wine and Grapes
Braised Celery with Sesame Seeds
Crisp Light Salad

Peach Mousse

Served with Semillon Chardonnay

PREPARATION TIMETABLE

1 day ahead: Prepare Potted Crab. Refrigerate. Make toast triangles to serve with Potted Crab. Store in an airtight container. Prepare chicken stock. Cover and refrigerate.

6 hours ahead: Prepare spatchcocks. Prepare first stage of Red Wine Sauce. Cover and refrigerate. Prepare Peach Mousse. Cover and refrigerate. Chill white wine.

1 hour ahead: Prepare salad and make dressing. Prepare garnishes.

30 minutes ahead: Cook spatchcocks.

Keep warm in oven. Cook celery and capsicum. Toast sesame seeds. Set aside.

15 minutes ahead: Complete preparation of Red Wine Sauce. Cook Braised Celery.

Time for dinner: Decorate Potted Crab with dill sprigs. Arrange spatchcocks on a serving platter. Toss salad with dressing. Garnish food and serve.

Dessert: Spoon mousse into serving glasses. Garnish and serve.

Grilled Spatchcocks with Red Wine and Grapes, Braised Celery with Sesame Seeds, Crisp Light Salad

POTTED CRAB WITH TOAST TRIANGLES

200 g canned crab, drained
1 teaspoon lemon juice
1 tablespoon chopped chives
½ cup mayonnaise
2 tablespoons thickened cream
pinch curry powder
3 teaspoons gelatine dissolved in 1
    tablespoon water
lemon zest and dill sprigs for serving

Blend together crabmeat, lemon juice and chives. Fold in mayonnaise, cream, curry powder and dissolved gelatine. Spoon into prepared moulds and chill. When ready to serve, unmould and garnish with lemon zest and dill sprigs. Serve with toast triangles.

GRILLED SPATCHCOCKS WITH RED WINE AND GRAPES

2 spatchcocks (poussins), halved and
    backbones removed
30 g butter, melted
squeeze lemon juice
salt and pepper

Red Wine Sauce
backbones from birds
1 tablespoon vegetable oil
½ an onion, chopped
¼ cup red grapes, chopped
¼ teaspoon thyme
½ small bay leaf
½ cup dry fruity red wine
¾ cup chicken stock
8 red grapes, halved and seeded
8 seedless green grapes, halved
1 teaspoon Dijon mustard
2 teaspoons butter

Brush spatchcocks with melted butter and lemon juice. Sprinkle with salt and pepper and set aside.

To make the sauce: brown backbones in oil. Saute onion and chopped red grapes lightly until light brown in colour. Add thyme, bay leaf, wine and chicken stock. Bring to boil and simmer to reduce to ⅔ cup. Strain stock, cover and chill.

To cook spatchcocks, cook under a hot grill skin side down 4–5 minutes, frequently brushing with basting liquid. Turn, baste and grill a further 6 minutes. Longer time may be required depending on size of bird. Test with a skewer. Juices will run clear when cooked.

To complete the sauce, soften red and green grape halves in butter. Stir in reserved stock and cooking juices from spatchcocks and cook gently till reduced and slightly thickened. Whisk in mustard.

Serve the spatchcocks on a platter dressed with grape clusters and a little sauce. Serve rest of sauce separately.

BRAISED CELERY WITH SESAME SEEDS

½ bunch celery, sliced diagonally
½ red capsicum (pepper), seeded and
    cut into thin strips
1 tablespoon oil
1 teaspoon sesame oil
1 clove garlic, crushed
toasted sesame seeds for serving

Parboil celery and capsicum 1–2 minutes in a saucepan of boiling water. Drain.

Heat oil and cook garlic 1 minute. Add celery and capsicum. Cook over high heat 4–6 minutes, stirring constantly. Remove celery with a slotted spoon and transfer to a serving dish. Serve sprinkled with some toasted sesame seeds.

CRISP LIGHT SALAD

1 fennel bulb and heart
½ Chinese cabbage
2 stalks celery
2 shallots
1 tablespoon fine slivers preserved
    Chinese ginger in syrup
2 tablespoons vinaigrette dressing
    mixed with 1 teaspoon preserved
    ginger syrup

Trim fennel bulb, remove outer sheath and slice in very fine rings. Shred Chinese cabbage. Slice shallots and celery into fine diagonal strips.

Mix all together with slivers of ginger. Cover and chill.

Toss salad with dressing just before serving.

Peach Mousse

PEACH MOUSSE

2 ripe peaches
1 tablespoon lemon juice
almond or orange liqueur (optional)
1 cup cream, chilled
2 egg whites
¼ cup sugar
Amaretti biscuits, for garnish

Blanch peaches in boiling water for 1 minute. Remove, plunge into cold water then carefully peel. Slice peaches and puree in food processor with lemon juice and liqueur.

Beat the cream until stiff and chill.

Beat egg whites until stiff peaks form, gradually adding the sugar until glossy. Fold the whipped cream and meringue mixtures into the peach puree.

Spoon mousse into custard cups or glasses. Freeze 1 hour then transfer to refrigerator for 2 hours. Serve chilled but not hard, garnished with Amaretti.

LIGHT AND DELICIOUS DINNER FOR FOUR

During the summer months people are more aware of what they are eating. Keeping a watchful eye on weight is one consideration. The other is that more entertaining — and consequently more eating — is done during the warmer weather. This light dinner of delicate foods in small helpings will entice your guests.

MENU

Fish with Brandy Cream

Lambs' Brains with Cucumber Salad
Fettuccine with Prawns and Peas

Mango and Kiwifruit Sorbet

Served with Chardonnay

PREPARATION TIMETABLE

1 day ahead: Prepare Mango and Kiwifruit Sorbet. Prepare fish stock, cover and refrigerate.
6 hours ahead: Prepare silver dory fillets and slice shallots. Soak lambs' brains. Prepare sauce, shrimp and vegetables for fettuccine. Cover and refrigerate. If serving fettuccine cold, cook, cool and then combine all ingredients. Refrigerate. Chill beverages.
3 hours ahead: Cook lambs' brains.
1 hour ahead: Prepare Brandy Cream Sauce. Cover and set aside. Prepare Lambs' Brains with Cucumber Salad. Refrigerate. Make vinaigrette dressing.
30 minutes ahead: Prepare garnish for sorbet.
15 minutes ahead: Cook silver dory fillets. Reheat sauce. Garnish and serve immediately. If serving fettuccine hot, cook and reheat sauce. Combine all ingredients. Garnish and serve. Chill sorbet glasses.
Time for dinner: Dress salad and serve.

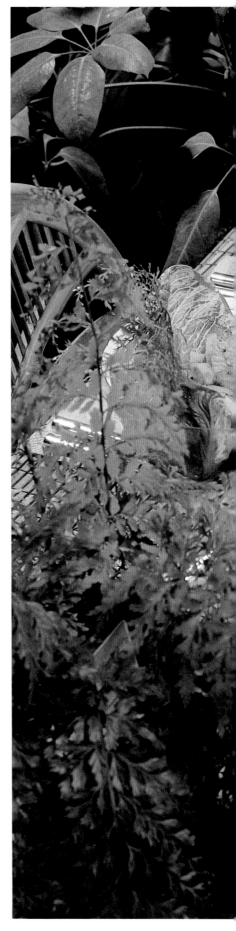

Fish with Brandy Cream
Fettuccine with Prawns and Peas,
Lambs' Brains with Cucumber Salad

FISH WITH BRANDY CREAM

4 fillets silver dory (or whiting)
40 g butter
3 shallots, sliced
1 bouquet garni
1 cup fish stock
salt and white pepper
2 teaspoons flour
¼ cup dry white wine
¼ cup cream
1 tablespoon brandy
1 teaspoon French mustard
1 tablespoon snipped chives

Cut the silver dory into 1 cm wide strips.

Melt half the butter in a heavy-based frying pan with a lid. Add shallots, reserving about 1 tablespoon, and fry over a low heat until soft. Add bouquet garni, fish stock and fish. Season, cover and simmer gently for 3–5 minutes. Carefully lift the fish from the pan, set aside and keep warm. Strain cooking liquid, reserving ½ cup.

In a clean pan, melt remaining butter. Add remaining shallots and cook. Add flour and cook, stirring, for 1 minute. Remove pan from heat and gradually add wine. Simmer the sauce until reduced by a quarter. Add reserved fish stock, bring to boil and simmer for 5 minutes. Stir in cream, brandy and mustard.

Arrange fish on 4 serving plates. Spoon over the sauce, garnish with chives and serve.

Fettuccine with Prawns and Peas,
Lambs' Brains with Cucumber Salad

LAMBS' BRAINS WITH CUCUMBER SALAD

4 sets of lambs' brains, soaked for 2 hours in water, rinsed and soaked again
small piece onion
1 tablespoon lemon juice
salt and pepper
1 cucumber
mustard cress
2 tablespoons parsley, finely chopped

Vinaigrette Dressing
1 tablespoon wine vinegar
3 tablespoons vegetable oil
½ teaspoon mustard seeds
salt and pepper

Garnish
1 tablespoon capers
2 tablespoons pine nuts, toasted
mignonette (or soft head) lettuce leaves

Place brains in a saucepan of water and bring to boil very slowly. Remove brains immediately and plunge into cold water. Remove skin and membrane. Cook brains in fresh water with onion, lemon juice, salt and pepper for 5 minutes or until just firm. Do not allow to discolour and harden. Drain, cool and slice.

Peel cucumber, cut in half lengthways, remove seeds and slice into crescents.

Combine brains and cucumber in a bowl, snip cress and toss with parsley. Grind fresh pepper over salad. Dress with vinaigrette and garnish with capers and pine nuts.

Serve on mignonette lettuce cups on individual plates.

FETTUCCINE WITH PRAWNS AND PEAS

500 g cooked fettuccine, drained and kept warm
1 shallot, chopped
500 g cooked prawns, peeled and veins removed
1 cup cooked green peas
8 snow peas (mangetout), blanched and refreshed, for garnish

Sauce
2 egg yolks
1 tablespoon white wine vinegar
½ tablespoon fresh lemon juice
½ tablespoon finely chopped ginger root
salt and pepper
1 tablespoon hot water
⅓ cup olive oil
1 tablespoon sesame oil
¼ cup cream

To make the sauce: combine the egg yolks, vinegar, lemon juice, ginger, salt and pepper in blender. Add hot water and oils in thin stream. Add cream in thin stream and blend until combined.

In bowl, combine fettuccine, shallot, prawns and peas with sauce. Garnish with snow peas.

MANGO AND KIWIFRUIT SORBET

1 ripe mango, peeled, stoned and sliced
6 kiwifruit, peeled and sliced
1¼ cups sugar syrup (see note below)
1 tablespoon orange juice

Puree the mango and kiwifruit in a food processor. Add sugar syrup and orange juice. Blend well. Pour mixture into ice tray. Freeze 1 hour until ice crystals form. Remove and beat in food processor. Pour mixture back into ice tray and freeze. □

Just before serving, spoon into chilled glasses with extra slices of the 2 fruits for garnish.

Note: To make sugar syrup, dissolve 1 cup sugar in 1 cup water and bring to boil. Remove from heat, cool and store, covered in refrigerator until needed.

Mango and Kiwifruit Sorbet

WINTER GET-TOGETHER ROUND THE FIRE FOR EIGHT

This winter dinner has an Austro-Hungarian flavour. Starting with a warming Oyster Soup it goes on to veal, with a Haricot Bean Goulash and Carrots and Sour Cream, served with crusty bread. Apple Strudel has been chosen as a fitting finale for this dinner party.

MENU

Oyster Soup

Veal Fillets
Haricot Bean Goulash
Carrots in Sour Cream
Poppy Seed Plaits

Apple Strudel

Served with Cabernet Shiraz

PREPARATION TIMETABLE

Prepare ahead and freeze: Haricot Bean Goulash.

1 day ahead: Prepare fish stock and croutons for Oyster Soup. Prepare and cook Haricot Bean Goulash. Refrigerate in a covered container. Slice carrots for Carrots in Sour Cream. Refrigerate in a plastic bag. Prepare and bake Poppyseed Plaits. Cool and store in an airtight container until ready to reheat.

6 hours ahead: Prepare Veal Fillets up to the stage of pan frying. Place on a tray, cover and refrigerate. Prepare Tomato Sauce to serve with Veal Fillets. Cover with plastic wrap and refrigerate until ready to reheat. Boil rice, cool, cover and refrigerate until ready to reheat.

3 hours ahead: Prepare and set aside individual ingredients for Oyster Soup. Prepare garnishes. Prepare Apple Strudel filling. Refrigerate in a covered container.

1 hour ahead: Complete preparation of Apple Strudel. Place on a greased baking tray. Cover and set aside.

30 minutes ahead: Complete preparation of Oyster Soup. Stir in cream and heat through at last minute. Fry Veal Fillets. Keep warm in a low oven. Reheat rice in oven. Cook Carrots in Sour Cream.

15 minutes ahead: Steam asparagus to accompany Veal Fillets. Reheat Tomato Sauce. Reheat Haricot Bean Goulash in saucepan. Warm Poppy Seed Plaits in oven. Bake Apple Strudel.

Time for dinner: Serve soup in individual bowls and top with croutons. Fluff up rice with a fork. Garnish dishes and serve.

Dessert: Place Apple Strudel on serving plate. Dust with icing sugar, cut into slices and serve.

Clockwise from top right: Oyster Soup, Haricot Bean Goulash, Veal Fillets, Carrots in Sour Cream, Poppy Seed Plaits.

Oyster Soup

OYSTER SOUP

60 g butter
1 onion, chopped
2 rashers bacon, rind removed and
  chopped
1.5 litres fish stock
½ cup finely chopped parsley
½ teaspoon curry powder
1 clove garlic, crushed
2 jars oysters, drained (about 40
  oysters)
600 mL cream
croutons, for serving

Melt the butter in a large saucepan, add the onion, bacon and garlic and cook until the onion has softened.

Add the stock, parsley and curry powder, bring to the boil and simmer uncovered for 10 minutes. Reduce the heat, add the oysters and cook for 10 minutes without boiling. Stir in the cream and heat through.

Serve with croutons.

VEAL FILLETS

16 veal fillet slices
1 egg, lightly beaten
flour and breadcrumbs for coating

Mushroom Filling
1 cup thick white sauce
1 cup button mushrooms, sliced
2 tablespoons cream
squeeze lemon juice
1 tablepoon white wine
salt and freshly ground pepper
100 g butter

Tomato Sauce
20 g butter, melted
1 tablespoon onion, chopped
1 clove garlic, finely chopped
2 tablespoons tomato paste
½ cup beef stock
3 ripe tomatoes, peeled, seeded and
  finely diced
salt

Flatten veal fillets by pounding lightly with a meat mallot or rolling pin.

To make the mushroom filling, combine all the filling ingredients and mix well.

Spread the filling evenly on one side of 8 veal slices. Top with remaining 8 veal slices. Dust in flour, dip into the beaten egg coating well, and then into the fresh breadcrumbs. Chill for 1 hour until the crumb coating is firm.

Melt the butter in a large frying pan over a high heat. Add the veal and cook for 6–8 minutes on each side turning once.

To make the sauce, melt the butter in a saucepan, add onion and garlic and fry for 4 minutes or until tender. Add tomato paste, stock, tomatoes and salt to taste. Simmer, stirring occasionally for 5 minutes. Spoon sauce over the veal before serving.

HARICOT BEAN GOULASH

1¼ cups dried haricot beans, soaked overnight
3 tablespoons oil
500 g onions, sliced
2 cloves garlic, crushed
2 large green capsicums (peppers), sliced
350 g zucchini (courgettes), sliced
250 g hot Hungarian salami (csabai), sliced
800 g canned tomatoes in juice
3 tablespoons tomato paste
1–2 tablespoons paprika
1 teaspoon sugar

Drain soaked beans, cover with water, bring to boil and simmer 1 hour till tender. Drain.

Heat oil and saute onion and garlic till soft. Add green capsicum and saute 2 minutes, stir in zucchini and csabai and saute further 2 minutes. Add beans to pan with remaining ingredients and season to taste.

Simmer uncovered for 20 minutes. Serve piping hot.

CARROTS IN SOUR CREAM

30 g butter
6 carrots, sliced thinly
juice half lemon
grated nutmeg
⅓ cup sultanas
⅔ cup sour cream
salt and pepper
chopped parsley

Melt butter and add carrots. Cover pan and saute gently 20 minutes until carrots are tender.

Stir in lemon juice, nutmeg, sultanas and sour cream, season to taste and heat through gently.

Serve immediately sprinkled with chopped parsley.

POPPY SEED PLAITS

6 cups flour
2 teaspoons salt
1 tablespoon butter or margarine
1½ teaspoons sugar
6 teaspoons compressed yeast or 2 sachets dried
200 mL lukewarm water
200 mL lukewarm milk
milk to glaze
poppy seeds

Sieve flour and salt into bowl, rub in butter and add sugar.

Blend yeast with milk and water, add to flour and mix to a firm dough.

Knead dough on lightly floured board until smooth and elastic, approximately 10 minutes. Divide dough into two, forming each piece into a ball. Place in greased bowls, cover and leave in warm place to double in bulk.

Punch down 1 ball of dough. Knead until smooth and elastic. Divide into 3 and roll each into a long sausage shape. Starting from the middle, plait pieces together, working towards one end. Turn dough around and plait other end. Pinch ends together to seal.

Proceed with second ball of dough, repeating process. Place loaves on greased baking trays, cover and leave in warm place till doubled in bulk, approximately 30 minutes.

Preheat oven to 200°C (400°F). Brush loaves with milk and sprinkle with poppy seeds. Bake 30–45 minutes until golden brown and sounding hollow when tapped.

APPLE STRUDEL

10 sheets filo pastry
125 g butter, melted
1 cup breadcrumbs
4 apples, peeled, cored and chopped
⅔ cup raisins
½ cup chopped walnuts
1 teaspoon cinnamon or mixed spice
¼ cup rum or grated rind and juice 1 lemon
½ cup caster sugar
½ cup milk
¼ cup icing sugar

Brush 5 sheets of filo pastry with melted butter, placing 1 on top of the other. Set aside. Repeat with remaining pastry sheets and set aside separately, covered with damp tea towel.

Scatter breadcrumbs over first layer of pastry, and then spread chopped apple, raisins, chopped walnuts, spices and rum (or lemon rind and juice). Sprinkle sugar over mixture.

Place second layer of pastry over the fruit. Roll strudel up and place on greased baking sheet. Brush top with milk.

Preheat oven to 200°C (400°F). Bake strudel for 30 minutes. Place on serving dish and dust with icing sugar. Cut into slices and serve warm. □

Apple Strudel

COOK AHEAD — FREEZER TO TABLE FOR SIX

Clever cooks fill their freezers with completed meals, sauces, desserts, stocks and pastries. The following Cook Ahead Dinner can be prepared well in advance and frozen, ready and waiting for an impromptu dinner party or gathering.

MENU

Belgian Leek Soup

Braised Rabbit Casserole
Carrots and Almonds
Sultana Pilaf

Grape and Wine Custard

Served with a Shiraz Mataro

PREPARATION TIMETABLE

Prepare ahead and freeze: Belgian Leek Soup — Prepare and cook up to the stage of adding cream. Freeze in a covered plastic container. Braised Rabbit Casserole — Prepare and cook completely. Freeze in a covered container. Carrots and Almonds — Bake 10 minutes, bar the addition of chopped almonds. Freeze.

1 day ahead: Prepare Sultana Pilaf and store as recipe states. Remove Braised Rabbit Casserole and Belgian Leek Soup from freezer and thaw in refrigerator.

6 hours ahead: Remove Carrots and Almonds from freezer. Thaw in refrigerator until ready to re-heat. Toast French bread, cover and set aside. Soak grapes for Grape and Wine Custard. Prepare custard. Refrigerate.

3 hours ahead: Chop almonds for Carrots and Almonds. Set aside. Prepare garnishes.

1 hour ahead: Froot grapes and chill until ready to garnish dessert.

30 minutes ahead: Reheat Sultana Pilaf and Braised Rabbit Casserole in the oven. Open red wine and allow to breathe.

15 minutes ahead: Reheat Leek Soup, adding cream. Sprinkle Carrots and Almonds with chopped almonds and reheat in oven.

Time for dinner: Garnish dishes and serve.

Dessert: Frost glass rims. Divide brandied grapes between glasses. Pour over custard — Garnish and serve.

Clockwise from top right: Sultana Pilaf, Belgian Leek Soup, Carrots and Almonds, Braised Rabbit Casserole

BELGIAN LEEK SOUP

40 g butter
250 g leeks
500 g potatoes, diced
1.5 litres beef stock
1 teaspoon salt
½ cup cream
6 slices toasted French bread
nutmeg
thin slices of leek for garnish

Heat butter and fry leeks gently for 3 minutes. Add diced potatoes, beef stock and salt and bring to the boil. Cover with lid, reduce heat and simmer for 40 minutes, stirring occasionally.☐

Before serving, stir in cream. Place one piece of toast in each soup bowl and pour over the hot soup. Sprinkle lightly with nutmeg and thin slices of leek.

BRAISED RABBIT CASSEROLE

2 rabbits, soaked 2 hours in salted water
200 g lean bacon, finely chopped
½ teaspoon salt
½ teaspoon ground pepper
3 tablespoons flour
3 leeks, sliced thinly
1 clove garlic
1 cup chicken stock
1 cup dry red wine
3 tablespoons brandy
1 tablespoon red-currant jelly
herbs in muslin bag: 1 crushed bay leaf, fresh rosemary sprigs, fresh lemon thyme sprigs and 5 crushed juniper berries
1½ tablespoons lemon juice
12 small pickling onions, parboiled and drained.

Drain wash and pat rabbits dry. Cut into serving pieces. Allow 2 pieces per person.

Cook bacon in a frying pan over moderate heat until crisp. Drain and reserve.

Sprinkle rabbit pieces with salt and pepper, dust with flour, brown in bacon fat and place in casserole. Reserve cooking juices.

Saute leeks and garlic to soften only. Add wine and stock and bring to boil. Add brandy, jelly and herb bag and reserved juices from rabbit. Pour liquid mixture over rabbit and sprinkle with bacon.

Cover and bake at 180°C (350°F) 1½ hours or until tender. If preferred, simmer gently on cooktop until tender.☐

Remove herb bag. Add lemon juice and correct seasonings. Add pickling onions 20 minutes before serving.

Braised Rabbit Casserole, Carrots and Almonds

CARROTS AND ALMONDS

2½ cups carrots, thinly sliced
1 small onion, chopped finely
1½ cups water
salt and cracked black pepper
1 tablespoon honey
2 tablespoons snipped dill
¼ cup sunflower seeds
1 egg, lightly beaten
⅓ cup almonds, chopped

Place carrots, onion, water and salt in saucepan. Bring to boil, cover and simmer until carrots are just tender.

Preheat oven to 180°C (350°F). Add all remaining ingredients except almonds to carrots; stir. Pour into shallow baking dish, sprinkle with almonds and bake 15 minutes. Serve hot.

SULTANA PILAF

2 cups long grain rice
30 g butter
1 onion, finely chopped
salt and pepper (optional)
4 cloves
3 cups boiling water
1 cup freshly squeezed orange juice
grated rind of 1 orange
60 g sultanas, soaked in boiling water

Rinse rice under cold running water. Drain well.

Melt butter in a heavy saucepan. Add onion and cook gently 5 minutes or until lightly browned. Add rice to the pan and stir to coat with butter. Season with salt and pepper. Add cloves and boiling water and bring to the boil. Lower the heat, adding orange juice. Cover tightly and cook over a low heat 20 minutes or

until rice has absorbed almost all the liquid and is tender. Uncover the pan and cook a further 1–2 minutes.

Stir orange rind and drained sultanas through the rice. Fluff up with a fork before serving.

If preparing ahead of time, spoon pilaf into a shallow casserole dish. Cool uncovered and then cover with plastic wrap or aluminium foil. Reheat before serving.

Grape and Wine Custard

GRAPE AND WINE CUSTARD

1¼ cups sweet white wine
grated rind 1 lemon
4 eggs, separated
½ cup caster sugar
2 tablespoons cornflour
3 tablespoons water
pinch salt
juice ½ lemon
250 g white muscat grapes
250 g black grapes
¼ cup brandy
1 egg white
¼ cup sugar

Boil white wine and lemon rind 2 minutes. Blend yolks with ½ the sugar. Mix cornflour with water and add to yolks. Gradually stir in hot wine. Cook in top of double saucepan over simmering water until thick, stirring all the time. Remove from heat.

Whisk whites and salt until stiff peaks form. Add rest of sugar and beat till thick. Fold in warmed custard with lemon juice.□

Reserve some grapes for decoration. Halve and seed remaining grapes and soak in brandy.

Beat egg white for garnish. Dip rims of 6 tall glasses first into beaten egg white, then into sugar. Dip reserved grapes into beaten egg white and sugar. Allow to dry and then chill.

Just before serving divide brandied grapes between glasses. Top up with custard mixture. Decorate with chilled frosted grapes.

INDEX